MW01108016

CDR Unlimited Publishing
P.O. Box 16141, Memphis TN 38186

Cover and Interior Design: Ambicionz
www.ambicionz.com

Disclaimer: This book is a compilation of stories from numerous experts who have each contributed a chapter. As such, the views expressed in each chapter are of those who submitted their stories.

Purpose Shakers — 1st ed.
ISBN 978-1540572240

Purpose Shakers

WOMEN WHO RISE TO THE CALL OF PURPOSE

Amazing Women Sharing Stories of Purpose

CDR UNLIMITED PUBLISHING
P.O. Box 16141
Memphis, TN 38186

Contents

Acknowledgement

I dedicate this book to my husband Cedric who is my greatest supporter, my daughters who consistently encourage me to continue the "Purpose" journey despite the obstacles I sometimes encounter, and each of the contributors included in this anthology for their "Purpose Shakers" visions, vocations, & victories!

Foreword

Purpose Shakers: Women Who Rise to the Call of Purpose reveals the true nature of a determined woman through the lives of many who have consistently shaken the purposes of others while remaining committed to their own purposes! Women are unique creatures who possess the ability to not only shake purpose but also birth multiple purposes, figuratively and naturally speaking!

I'm honored and blessed to be married to one of today's most influential "Purpose Shakers", Dr. C. Denise Richardson! She is the self-proclaimed, "quintessential purpose shaker" and, I'm thankful for her commitment to our daughters and women in general. Purpose Shakers is an inspirational, self-awareness book that challenges women to take an introspective look at their lives and the lives of those they influence. Dr. Richardson and her fellow contributors share intimate details of their lives that challenged and motivated them to become "purpose shakers". Purpose isn't free. The price attached to purpose costs dearly and, that price is sacrifice, persistence and hard work.

As I read through the pages of this collaboration, I realized that I too am a "Purpose Shaker"! No matter how difficult our childhoods may have been, we can always believe for an expected end. God began the good work in us and it is the same God who will complete it in us. These "purpose shakers" recognize the importance and potential of all women to "be"come all that God has predestined them to be!

Whether you were raised in poverty or wealth, education or illiteracy, single parent or both parents; you were created with a specific purpose and God's "ram in the bush" may be an unsuspecting "Purpose Shaker" to revive and restore what has been dormant. Congratulations to you for recognizing the importance you have in the lives of those you influence. You have made a wise investment in yourself and in your purpose through the purchase of this book!

Cedric D. Richardson

"Your passion definitely fuels the purpose within! Allow her to kick start your day...every day!"

C. Denise

Chapter 1

Developing Millennial Squads: A Purpose Concept

Dr. C. Denise Richardson

"When you realize God's purpose for your life isn't just about you, He will use you in a mighty way." - Tony Evans

I'm up early and excited today! It's the first week of school and I'm already anticipating the pre-freshman shenanigans from both the girls and the boys...albeit for different reasons! The cheerleaders are the best! They were selected in May and they've attended cheer camp! As we approach the 8 o'clock bell, I realize that my rosters for both preps are full! This should be an interesting year. The excitement of the day is matched only by my overwhelming fear of the unknown of what spiritual attacks I'd need to prepare for!

It was days like this that reminded me of "why" I attended a post-secondary institution of higher learning, of "why" I possibly disappointed my mother because I did not choose nursing as my career field, of "why" my experience with child sexual abuse caused me to demonstrate such a powerful sensitivity for women and girls. I realized that schools were breeding grounds for all forms of dysfunction, especially those I had experienced as a youth. Invariably, I would again attempt to "save" the youth.

My passion for inspiring girls made it easier for me as an educator on those days that I was overworked, underpaid, and under appreciated! Teaching is not only underrated but it is also overlooked as a top-ranking career field in regards to pay when compared with other career fields. Educating others is a calling, a ministry, a mandate that should not to be entered into without much prayer and research! The youth today are not reminiscent of the youth of a decade or more ago. It was my responsibility to awaken the purpose mandate in every student who was willing to listen. My purpose to share Christ in subtle yet definite ways with my students came at a great price. The price was my anonymity as a girls' and women's purpose advocate!

As a purpose advocate, it's always refreshing to deposit nuggets of wisdom, (self) love, and empathy (toward other women especially those who have potentially harmed us) into other women... both young and mature. The pain and fear that many young girls silently experience stems from a complex myriad of life experiences, people and thoughts. I've always believed that my purpose was greater than signing in to work in the mornings and signing out in the evenings. More than teaching core subject material for students to pass or fail standardized tests. More than a homework provider and 7-3. I am a woman who was called to promote purpose in girls and women.

"When you awaken purpose, she accomplishes much" - C. Denise

Welcome purpose! Many challenges, disappointments, heartbreaks and heartaches are certain to present themselves during the purpose journey! Do not become immensely despondent or especially discouraged. Authentic purpose advocates recognize the significance in overcoming potential barriers so that purpose thrives! If afforded the opportunity to thrive, purpose will not only thrive but also multiply in the lives of others! Purpose is contagious to those who desire to live a life of fulfillment and contentment. Otherwise, regret may take root. Once regret enters the heart or mind of an individual, it transforms into anger, envy, and covetousness.

Regret is a powerful emotion that lies just beneath the surface only to be revealed when we notice that we are unfulfilled in our lives. Regret indicators include the inability to celebrate others' achievements, inability to move forward in one's [own] purpose, lack of sincere support for other women who are in purpose. In many instances, our poor decisions directed our steps and guided our emotions and actions toward others! The Bible admonishes us to find something to do and do it! The "thing" we find to do should reveal purpose(s). And, once discovered and activated; we often find ourselves fulfilled to a certain degree.

Fulfillment will not be experienced or enjoyed to its greatest degree unless purpose prevails! Purpose allows the gifts and talents to flourish while blessing others. Purpose thrives in gifts rich in passion. Are your gifts passion rich? Do your gifts make room for you? Have you exposed your gifts to the fiery passion that fuels purpose! The practical role of purpose is the same for everyone. However, the manner in which each individual's purpose inspires another varies dramatically.

Awakening the purpose mandate in young people is both rewarding and beneficial. Inspiring purpose in others causes a chain reaction that requires action **NOW!** Once purpose is awakened, she refuses to be hushed, quieted, or stilled. She has a mission and that mission involves deliberate steps toward destiny. Purpose never procrastinates because she recognizes the significance of her presence in the lives of those who desire greatness!

Greatness, like success, is more subjective than objective. It's relative depending on who is defining it. One woman may view and define greatness as being a supportive wife, mother, and Christian. Whereas another may define greatness as her ability to climb the corporate ladder while impacting the lives of everyone she meets along the way. Still another may define greatness as contributing to her community in small yet tangible ways. One common factor connects each of these women's definition of greatness and it is "purpose".

Purpose requires one to identify the passion that draws them then, compels them to act! How amazing is that! No one's purpose is futile. Therefore, no one's journey to greatness can compare to anyone else's. The energy and effort you place into purpose reveals the degree of passion and your potential for greatness as it relates to destiny. Destiny is "that" place of full purpose! It's where everything that you've experienced, conquered, lived, and ultimately progressed toward since purpose was activated.

Activated purpose only signifies that we have become "aware" of a greater call or cause for which we were created. Keep in mind, all experiences in life (both negative and positive) "work together for good to them that love God, to them who are the called according to His purpose." Romans chapter eight reveals God's sovereignty in such a manner that leaves no question as to how believers should view the big picture of life as opposed to single pieces of that picture. God's plans for His children are both definite and purposeful as indicated in Jeremiah twenty-nine. What a blessing to know that all of our combined experiences (painful and rewarding) are part of God's plans for our lives! The experiences allow us the privilege to relate to someone else in authentic, relatable ways.

"Living in the shadow of another isn't purpose; its bondage" - C. Denise

Awakening the purpose mandate challenges each believer to become accountable for awakening not only her purpose but also the purposes of others, especially our children. It is incumbent upon each of us, as mature believers, to awaken the purpose mandate in youth while revealing its relevance to their world. The millennial's world is technological, financial, and image focused. It's no wonder the previous generation of believers appear intimidated or befuddled when purpose discussions arise. However, we must acknowledge and appreciate the mantle Jehovah has entrusted to us (our children)...to influence, to shape, to nurture in the fear and admonishment of the Lord our Creator. Nothing has changed as it relates to living our lives to glorify Him and it begins and ends in our homes. Purpose, like faith, begins now. What has God mandated you to do to facilitate or encourage purpose in another?

"The single greatest reason why we are losing a generation is because the home is no longer the place of the transference of the faith. We live in a day of 'outsourcing'...Today, we have a generation of people that outsource their kids." - Tony Evans

About the Author

Dr. C Denise Richardson, women's and children's abuse prevention proponent, humanitarian, community leader, freelance writer, author, Life Strategist, ordained minister, former public school educator, administrator and Ex. Director of CDR Unlimited, is a survivor of both child sexual abuse (CSA) and domestic violence (DV). C. Denise inspires women to confront personal and professional mountains in order to transform into women of prayer, power, purpose and prosperity! These four pillars correlate to individual and corporate legacies! C. Denise inspires women to activate/awaken purpose first in themselves and then others! #MountainMovers and #PurposeShakers are her most notable conferences. Dr. C. also offers monthly MastHERmind sessions for the aforementioned conference titles. Dr. C. loves women and is a radical catalyst for life, love, & legacy through accountability, faith, application, & collaboration!

C. Denise earned four degrees that include one undergrad, two masters, & one doctoral degree. Additionally, C. Denise enrolls in CEUs in education, psychology, and counseling courses annually. Her commendations include community activism with the homeless, socially disadvantaged, and abused. C. Denise is also a member of various, notable community organizations.

C. Denise, like many of her followers, has endured challenges, setbacks, and betrayals. However, she's also experienced triumphs, joys, and accomplishments. Dr. C. sis obsessed with seeing women encourage, support, and empower other women! It's her absolute favorite! She believes the world needs more of it! Because she is so passionate about women, she continues to offer life changing, mind altering courses that both challenge and support women's empowerment!

Dr. C. recognizes the significance of authenticity and accessibility! She acknowledges that she is no different than other women EXCEPT she opened the door to opportunity and that she has shared and continues to share her CSA and domestic abuse experiences unapologetically and unashamedly! She is passionate about her role in the lives of women! C. Denise partners with other women from various backgrounds, races, socioeconomic statuses, religions, & nationalities for the greater good of our world!

Dr. C. is married to Cedric Richardson (19 years) and, they work together in ministry, community, business, and family. They oversee both Life Changers Outreach Ministries Corporation (LCOMC), a 501(c)3 organization and Life Changers Church International (LCCI) in Memphis, TN. The central objective of this faith based ministry is to restore and reconcile families to Christ through the word of God. We do this through a number of methods including, but not limited to mentorship, individual and family counseling, life skill planning, literacy education, and computer and technology training. Three of their six daughters serve in various capacities of the aforementioned outreach.

www.cdrunlimited.com
C Denise Richardson: FB
@DrCDenise:Twitter & Instagram
richstrategist@gmail.com

"Allow NOONE to box your purpose, unless you're gifting it to assist others."

C. Denise

Chapter 2

Purpose Ignited: A Soul Awakening
Eugenia Gray

In Exodus 3:8, when God met Moses at the burning bush, He told him that He was going to deliver His people from bondage and into a land flowing with "milk and honey". Yet, we know when God delivered His people out of bondage, but He led them directly into a "wilderness" where they spent 40 years. We know that their wilderness experience had a purpose because the Bible tells us that there was a shorter route available that they could have taken and avoided the wilderness altogether. Exodus 13:17 says, "God did not lead them by the way of the land of the Philistines, even though it was near."

Have you ever had something unexplainable happen to you and you felt like no one, absolutely no one would understand? Well for me, in 2008 and into the first half of 2010, I made some significant changes in my life. I had what you would call an epiphany (a serious reality check)...because of an insightful and profound spiritual awakening. This awakening has affected every aspect of my life – my individuality, spirituality, finances, and even my relationships.

On a late Friday afternoon, I woke up to one helluva hangover! I looked in the mirror and asked myself, "What are you trying to prove and, who are you trying to prove it to?" Reluctantly, I answered to myself "That's the problem, I don't give a damn about proving anything to anybody!" I looked at the dresser in my bedroom, evidence of battling with myself, or the least, a version of me in some aspect. A broken mirror, my hair askew, a cut on the back of my hand, dried blood on my clothes and the stench of a much needed shower. For some odd reason, I was hearing those voices again, a baby crying, the distant utters of conversations, so vague it almost sounded as if it were in another language of some sort. I thought to myself – if I think I'm crazy, I know everyone else will too. As I looked around my house, things weren't where I'd left them; at least that's the way it appeared. Everything somehow looked different! There was so much noise and chaos in my head that I could feel my temples throbbing at a rapid pace. I looked in the mirror and almost didn't recognize myself. Of course I knew it was me, but not me in some sense. I kept staring at the face in the mirror with an anticipation that the blur of my face would clear up; similar to that of a camera's focus lens. For some strange reason, I could hear Big Mama telling me to speak loud and hard. The next thing I knew this loud screeching cry came out of my mouth, I felt faint as tears rolled down my face. I was wanting to give up, but for some strange reason I knew what was happening. Right there in my bedroom, was my place of reckoning.

The flashbacks started – just like in a movie when it's put in fast-forward mode. I could not only remember, but I could feel the emotions as I relived the moments. I could smell the aromas of every incident that flashed across my mind...breath, body odor, cologne, hair products and the like unlocked from my memory like the turning of a key. When the old bastard touched me, when they held me down, when he slapped me, when he hit me, when he pushed me down, when she cut my hair, when he walked away, when they called me those names, when he put me out. The things I swore to forget. As I held myself in the fetal position of my bedroom floor, I cried until I started moaning and then another set started flashing, except these were voices, shouting that I was unfit to live, I was good for nothing, I was free and easy, who would want you, you're nothing! Pretty, but not good enough, smart, but not worthy of anything. I swallowed all that I'd heard in my head and let it fester for maybe thirty minutes. I cried hard and long until my physical body couldn't stand it anymore. I rushed to the toilet to spew out the vomit of all that I'd allowed myself to succumb to. As I laid on the bathroom floor, I cried out Jesus to take away all these memories and the emotions that were connected. Make it go away, please. It was as if I'd crossed into another dimension. I found myself wishing I had a magic wand to either erase what I'd just experienced, or to somehow create a situation that was a little more soothing and comforting. Out of nowhere, I heard a voice saying one word – **FORGIVE!** What the hell? Never. Simply stated. I felt better in knowing that I had some form of hate deep in my spirit. For years I knew it was there, but dormant. Unbothered. It didn't mess with me and I didn't disturb it. So when I could make clear sense of what I was hearing I realized that as simple as is sounds to forgive, I had to go through the process.

After that realization, I knew I had to give up wholeheartedly of myself. Forgiving is the most painful dissecting of the spirit. But I somehow knew I had to do this – I had a lot of people to forgive. The rapist, the abuser, the jealous woman, the childhood bullies, the molesters, both my Mom and Dad. Everyone. I was mad at so many people, I lost count. But I couldn't forget being mad at myself. Regrets for not doing what was truly in my heart. Everything that I'd blocked revealed itself to me. This was pure agony.

But then something came over me as if I was wrapped in this invisible mixture of a chenille and fleece afghan. It wasn't for everyone else – well...it was for the most part, but I needed to forgive myself. First and foremost because in my heart I know I'd not been perfect, and that wasn't easy. Merely because we never see the wrong that we ourselves do. This mirror experience would change the rest of my life. After all, it was me who decided to give up what I wanted to be more concerned for what others wanted – even from me.

For years, I lived with this guilt. I'd hidden emotions, feelings, stirrings and yes I even grumbled quite a bit. I'd done such a good job of masking all that and I even went through my daily living of working, wifing and parenting as if I had it all together. I knew I could not be pretending to feel great about my life on the outside while feeling guilty about my life on the inside. I didn't let any of this steam-off. I just let it boil and simmer until an eruption of massive explosion will have to be reckoned with. Somehow, I knew that if I were to become a minister of God's word and a kingdom voice, I'd have to live my truth and teach from it. This challenge was personal – I also had to forgive myself. But I had no idea how to. This wasn't some life skills hack you find on the internet. It's very hard to forgive yourself when you haven't learned how to forgive others. In order for me to be effective with this "tool" forgiveness, I had to become one with God, become the master of my life, accept my anointing and create my destiny. The very thing that I never wanted to acknowledge, the very thing I kept running from. I had to exercise true worship and be totally in charge of everything that happens to me, even as Jesus did. This thing is hard to grasp. It's hard to try to emulate such a wonderful man's awesome level of forgiveness. Even through the midst of His crucifixion and His dying, He was able to ask God to forgive them. It's the highest, yet most painful exercising of spiritual igniting that one can exercise. So I stood there, staring. As the tears rolled down my face I uttered "I love you so much and I want you to know that I forgive you and I will give all of myself to ensure you live in your God-given purpose! Speak loud and hard and make me proud!"

I can now say that I am very excited about the course my life has taken. My life changes made an almost 360-degree turn for me, from my outer physical existence to my inner spiritual existence. I'm sure that many of you are going through great challenges too. And like me, you are facing the decision to make choices involving the call of your heart's desires and the call of the world. Just as I did, you are going to have to trust your inner feelings and intuition like you never have before. I also know that no matter what anyone else thinks, you had to do what was necessary – stop hearing and start listening!

Whenever God leads you somewhere, he has a purpose and a predestined place for you, even if the route is a long or a dry one. Often times, wilderness is the doorway to your destined purpose. At the initiation of Jesus' public ministry, He was led into the wilderness first before He ever preached a sermon. If you are in a wilderness right now, remember what you learned while there because it will be necessary to sustain you in your Promised Land. Don't faint or lose heart. You may be at the door of your promise and your purpose. You may not have been lost at all - you may have simply been led! Remember your purpose is stated in Genesis 1:28 *"Be fruitful, and multiply, and replenish the earth, and subdue it: and have dominion over every living thing that moveth upon the earth."*

I was a hesitant surrenderer because of fear - Spending most of my childhood years in the country, I was basically raised by my grandmother. My grandparents were successful as individuals. They lived long lives and enjoyed their retirement. My grandmother, an educator – my grandfather, a pastor and preacher of the word of God. As a child I was raised in the church and taught to always go to church. Sunday School, BTU summer sessions, Christian Camp, choir, and the like. Sometimes we'd sit down and dissect the scriptures and reference the depth of their meanings; a slick debater, that was me. But the absolute truth of my life had no connection whatsoever with being raised in the church. Because of my grandparents, we were in church 25/8! Yes, I said it – Sunday school, morning service, evening service, teacher meeting, prayer meeting, mission meeting, choir rehearsal, pastor's aide committee meetings, etc. Because of my prolific speaking abilities, my grandmother always had me on some brothers' or sisters' program or event. She'd always tell me before I spoke, "You better speak loud and hard, make me proud!" You see Big Mama was a socialite - in the community, on the education platform and in the church circles. So being her little trophy granddaughter was the cherry on her sundae. Whenever Granddaddy had to preach, she'd always drag me and my sister to church too. As I entered into my teens, I could feel myself rapidly burning out on church. I would find myself going more so out of obligation rather than actually knowing "who" God is and "what" He could've been to my life. I guess I had some things to learn.

For years, I dealt with stress and hardship of struggling through a divorce and being a single-parent. This was very painful as I didn't believe that anything good could possibly come from its after effects. It actually ripped our family apart, I felt like my life was ruined and a failure. Every single day was a struggle. I desperately wanted to give up. I didn't know how I could go on. I felt like my life was over, but it wasn't.

My faith in God allowed me to tap into an inner-strength deep within. It was almost like being led with a small light to my path.

I, just as many others, have found myself stuck in difficult situations often feel as if I've become lost with no purpose. With no warning, somehow I arrived in a wilderness where everything had dried up and nothing seemed to be growing. I had a great job, attended church, sang in the choir, participated in the PTA/PTO, dated occasionally and even enjoyed a little pampering. But I was smack dab in the middle of this vast emptiness for so long that I had given up on things changing and concluded that this must be all God has in store for me. On numerous occasions, I attempted to change my situation, but all efforts failed. Education wasn't enough, experience was too much. My marriage wasn't living, actually it had no life. My money was less than the bills and my spirit always seemed melancholy. As I tell you this story, you'll later find that I wasn't lost at all. But where I was, was squarely within the "will" of God. All my dry places in life weren't the result of being lost. Sometimes God uses dry places as a place of preparation for your purpose. All of this was my purpose preparation!

You see, the night before, I had asked God that if there was really something for me to do that'd help someone else what would He have me to do. Then I kept remembering every time my grandfather would tell me you're going to be a preacher, marry a preacher or be a politician in some sort of way. I would regularly say, "No, no...not me!" He would say "why not you?" I know I'm supposed to do something that required me running my mouth. Please...I was supposed to be a lawyer!! But life dealt me a different hand. At this point I'd decided that I wanted to be the best person I knew to be. The only thing that kept getting in my way was fear. I'm not sure how everyone else deals with it, but for me, when I became a speaker, I started listening, even to fear. Thus the **IGNITING!** The realization that I was born to succeed! Expressing what was holding me from moving forward in life into a joyful and fulfilling world of "more than enough." Developing my spirit of purpose, was the key to overcoming all the blocks in front of me – my finances, family problems, emotional stress, depression, addiction, career concerns and yes, even me! Once I could truly forgive, I saw myself and recognized my purpose and entered into

God's supernatural destiny designed uniquely for me. And yes, this could've be a different ending. Stay tuned...that's another story.

About the Author

In her private practice consultancy, Allegis Development Group, LLC, Eugenia conceptualizes and implements strategic resolutions to business planning, marketing, branding development, communications strategies, and publicity initiatives for a myriad of multifaceted clients. She is the founder of Anointed Destiny Ministries and recently launched Next Level Forward Success Strategies, LLC, a women's empowerment consultancy focused on personal and business strategies for success in life, relationships, finances and personal development to live a purposed life. Eugenia takes pleasure, through the love of God, in sharing her own life experiences and traumatic ordeals with others to break free from the pains of their past; she facilitates "Intellectual Thought Conferences" where she touches the lives of those who have been trapped by abandonment, neglect, rejection, molestation and other abuses. She's an entrepreneur, community thought leader, a sought after dynamic speaker and soon to be author of "The Echo of God's Whisper," and the blog "Essentially Empowered" both to be released soon.

Eugenia has a strong mandate and special calling to uplift and empower life application strategies for new life and success by teaching spiritual health & healing, and successful business strategies. Her mission in life is to transform lives, heal hearts, empower minds and win souls for Christ. Eugenia works with coaches, speakers, authors and entrepreneurs to develop income by utilizing a system that gives you tools to effectively meet the needs of those served.

"Take time to focus on your [individual] purpose. Now, write down in practical yet applicable details how you can begin to live a more purposeful life."

C. Denise

Chapter 3

Purpose in Progress: One Woman's Journey to Destiny!

Chiquita Mays

My defining purpose moment came at a time in my life when seemingly everything was going well. On the surface I appeared to be a highly successful corporate executive who worked diligently to advance. As the first Black female electrical engineer to work in new product development for the leading office manufacturer seventeen years of climbing the corporate ladder seemed to pay off well. Finding myself in hotels in different cities leading continuous improvement projects and calling home to read to my children. More and more my children were beginning to know me less and less as "Mommy" and I was missing valuable moments in their young lives.

More and more I began to long to be "Mommy" and still have a career; work life balance was far from reach. While my husband was not complaining overtly we had become passersby as we were consumed by 12 to 14-hour work days. One night when one of our girls yelled from her bedroom for Daddy to pray I broke down in tears as I realized my children did not even call out to me! Through my tears I searched for a journal that held goals long recorded. Recalling the goal to start my own business by age 40 gave new life to my purpose! I soon sat down with Willie and began to draft a two-year plan to leave corporate America and start CLM Consulting Professionals LLC. It took rediscovering and reigniting my purpose to fuel my journey into destiny!

What is your life's purpose? What is the objective of your life? What is the divine destiny of God for your life? No matter the purpose for which God created you; this purpose will not happen overnight! Life is the cumulative journey of your purpose! Your purpose is a work in process, you are a work in process. You are God's work in process! God designed your life to live out the purpose for which He created you!

Romans 8:28 King James Version (KJV)

28 And we know that all things work together for good to them that love God, to them who are the called according to his purpose.

We are prompted by the Word of God to understand every circumstance, situation, or event transpires to work the purpose for which God has called you. God-given purpose is accomplished throughout the course of life. You are called to live out purpose daily, moment by moment. You must understand accomplishing purpose will require a lifetime. Your life's work after discovering your God-designed purpose is to dedicate your life to accomplish that purpose! The life that pleases God is one lived on purpose!

Matt 25:19-21; 24-26 King James Version

19 After a long time the lord of those servants cometh, and reckoneth with them.

20 And so he that had received five talents came and brought other five talents, saying, Lord, thou deliverest unto me five talents: behold, I have gained beside them five talents more.

21 His lord said unto him, Well done, thou good and faithful servant: thou hast been faithful over a few things, I will make thee ruler over many things: enter thou into the joy of thy lord.

24 Then he which had received the one talent came and said, Lord, I knew thee that thou art an hard man, reaping where thou hast not sown, and gathering where thou hast not strawed:

25 And I was afraid, and went and hid thy talent in the earth: lo, there thou hast that is thine.

26 His lord answered and said unto him, Thou wicked and slothful servant, thou knewest that I reap where I sowed not, and gather where I have not strawed:

Recall the story of the servants with the talents. The husbandman entrusted talents or valuable gifts to his servants. Upon his return he finds the servants who received the most talents had also done the most with those talents! The servant to whom he provided the least talents hid the little talent given to him. The husbandman is infuriated and gives the talent to the servant whom demonstrated the best stewardship of the talents. Our life's are likened unto the servants and the talents.

Our Savior has left us here on earth and He has returned to heaven; however, He left each and every one a measure of faith and gifts, talents, or a purpose! Individual purpose is provided given our several abilities. The Husbandman will return for each of His servants one day and will then determine how each utilized the talents or their purpose. The time of His return may vary for each servant; what is established is the expectation the talents have been put to good use and have grown. The Father God is looking for a return on investment for the life and purpose He has given.

Purpose is Accomplished On Purpose

Your life's purpose will not happen overnight and is not accidental. Accomplishing your God-given purpose is your life's work. You are to commit your life to God and in obedience fulfill His purpose. This is not an accidental nor coincidental work! You must commit yourself to live on purpose; to live in purpose; to live for purpose; and to live out your purpose! Daily we are surrounded by those who seemingly have no purpose or have not discovered their purpose. We must not take for granted that purpose will automatically take place. Purpose requires our deliberate effort and focus. Purpose is accomplished on purpose!!! It requires a purposeful effort.

Your life was called into existence for a specific purpose and your life should be lived to accomplish this purpose. Whatever your purpose, accomplishing it will require you to live on purpose. Purpose must never be left to chance. You must be deliberate in your pursuit of purpose. You must now accept two eternal truths concerning your purpose:

1. Purpose is not accomplished accidentally.
2. Purpose is a lifelong and continuous process (journey).

Purpose provides meaning and usefulness for life and is never accomplished accidentally. Circumstances may at times appear accidental; however, remember God was working it out for His purpose all along!

Olympic track star, Wilma Rudolph, suffered a life plagued with illness from birth often impacting her legs. The famous sprinter was born premature and would be forced to wear a leg brace after a bout with polio and scarlet fever. Seemingly these injuries and illnesses would prevent the young woman from becoming the then known, fastest woman on earth! Rudolph is known for training for hours every day to perfect her skills as a basketball player and a runner. This purposeful and determined training led to the strengthening of her legs and her discovery by a well-known track coach. This woman who suffered a crippling disease would go on to win three gold medals for track! She did not trust her life's purpose to chance and coincidence; she made deliberate daily efforts to achieve her life's purpose! Had she allowed her circumstances to dictate her purpose she would not have become known as the fastest woman on earth. Her relentless pursuit compelled her training routine.

Your life's purpose should dictate your daily routine! You must develop a routine and goals in alignment with your purpose. Purpose is not a destination; it is a process! In the business world we understand a process is a series of steps performed on specific inputs to produce a desired output. In other words, you put something in and you get something out. To accomplish your purpose, you must first put something into your purpose. Then you must perform some action or task. Finally, you will receive some output. The servants with the most talents and Wilma Rudolph performed deliberate action towards their purpose daily. For their effort they receive tremendous rewards.

It is a process: a lifelong and continuous process! So many people wander through life with no purpose and daily waste that great potential they were created to accomplish. The process will require deliberate action from you; this is not an accidental journey. The process ends when your purpose is wasted or exhausted! When you have exhausted energy with no purpose the process ends. When you have lived out every ounce of purpose, your life's journey or process will end! Live a life filled with purpose! Leave a life fueled with purpose! Leave a legacy fulfilled on purpose!

About the Author

Chiquita L Mays is business woman, author, career and development coach, publisher, pastor, and public speaker. Chiquita called on her educational background as an electrical engineer and extensive work experience in engineering, lean manufacturing, process improvement, and leader development when she founded CLM Consulting Professionals LLC in November 2008.

Chiquita Mays is an engineer and training and development professional who is dedicated to the continuous improvement of people, leadership, processes, and organizations. She has more than 20 years of experience in product development, manufacturing processes, lean systems, quality systems, training, and leadership development.

She completed her BSE in Electrical Engineering at North Carolina Agricultural and Technical State University and began a career in new product development and design for Steelcase in Grand Rapids, Michigan. She would hold positions in testing, R&D, building codes & approvals, and quality before transitioning to production supervision and lean management. Chiquita received her certification in Lean Systems from the University of Michigan and also obtained a Green belt in Six Sigma. She became a Lean Manager and assumed responsibility for the training and development initiatives in the organization. Her specializations became Lean/Six Sigma and leadership development.

In November 2008, Chiquita left the organization and launched CLM Consulting Professionals LLC, a company that would carry out her vision of total and sustainable development. Since that time CLM has worked with hundreds of corporations, municipalities, and organizations on development. CLM applies a holistic approach to development with an engineering division that helps their clients build robust processes while training and developing the leadership and people to maintain and continuously improve those processes. CLM also has a financial services division providing tax preparation and insurance services with offices now in multiple locations.

Chiquita has a Master's degree in industrial and organizational psychology from Capella University. She is currently pursuing a doctorate in the same discipline. Her dissertation like her thesis is centered on transformational leadership. She serves faithfully along with her husband as pastors of No Limits Christian Church in Georgia. Chiquita is a best-selling author and travels extensively for speaking engagements.

"Today, awaken purpose to a revised plan of action. Renegotiate the "terms of the contract" with your purpose! You can do it! You'll appreciate "you" later!"

C. Denise

Chapter 4

There is Purpose in the Whispers

Teresa Velardi

"After the earthquake came a fire, but the Lord was not in the fire. And after the fire came a gentle whisper." 1 Kings 19:12

What if you paid attention to that little voice that whispered to you when you are at a crossroad in your life? What if you actually moved in the direction you were guided to go? Do you believe that your life is divinely inspired and the whispers are the breath of God? I do.

There have been several times in my life I have heard those whispers. Some of them, I paid attention to, others I ignored, thinking I knew the way and my decisions were the right ones. I will be the first to encourage you to listen to the whispers.

A Whisper of Warning

On that day most every woman dreams of, there were a multitude of signs that the wedding should never take place. I ignored the fact that the limo was an hour late, that the priest read the wrong passages and discard my spending hours looking for the perfect words. I ignored my mother's great intuition that this wasn't the man for me. Deep down, I knew she was right.

The church was full when I finally arrived. I stood in the back of the church, ready to walk down the aisle on the arm of my father. He'd gone to great lengths to look his best for this special moment. I am the oldest and only of his three daughters who chose to wed in church. He'd doubled up on dental appointments to make sure his smile was as bright as possible in the pictures he would cherish. He looked amazing in his tuxedo, and tears of joy filled his eyes as we waited for the music to begin.

I had a sick feeling in my stomach. I brushed it off as a side effect of the anxiety I'd experienced waiting for the limo to arrive. I took a deep breath. The music started and the bridal party began the walk down the aisle. First the bridesmaids and groomsmen, then the tiny steps of my niece spreading rose petals before the music changed to "Here Comes the Bride".

I saw every face on the way down that aisle; my friends, my family, my soon to be mother in law, each one with a smile on their face. They were excited to be there, and they were happy for me. But why wasn't I?

My Dad handed me to the groom after kissing me on the cheek and giving me a hug. It was time. That's when I realized the groom wasn't even present for the moment. He was high as a kite. Wasn't that the one thing I had asked for? Just be sober and drug free when we take our vows. I knew he had a problem, but I also believed all the promises he made that he would stop.

When I looked into his eyes, that sick feeling returned. I looked around the room. All eyes were on me. The priest began the ceremony. The words he spoke weren't the ones I had chosen. No one would know except me. Wasn't this supposed to be one of the most special days of my life? And the priest is reading the wrong scriptures. The feeling in my stomach got worse. I did my best to let it go.

It came time for the vows. Oh no! "Teresa", the priest said, "Do you take this man to be your wedded husband?" Everything was a blur. All I heard was the voice that whispered inside "Teresa, don't do this." As the priest waited for my answer, I looked around the room. Again, I saw all the faces, my father, with his brilliant smile, my sisters, and my mother. She knew, my mother knew! I saw it on her face. She knew that I was finally having thoughts that this might not be the right thing for me. I turned back to the priest; he was looking impatient. He had warned me about being late and now I was dawdling with the most important part of the ceremony. He asked again. "Do you, Teresa, take this man to be your wedded husband?" I heard it again. "Teresa, don't do this. I have something so much better for you."

What should I do? All these people travelled to be at my wedding. How could I say no? What about the reception? What about the money we had spent on the catering? Money we didn't have. How could I just walk away? The feeling in my stomach got worse and the whisper seemed like a scream. I said "I do", and the emptiness hit me. It felt like the life had been sucked out of me. At that moment, I became one of the walking dead. I'd sold my soul for a wedding band.

The drinking and drugging got worse, and the alcoholic, drug addicted man I chose to marry, despite the whispered urge to not do so, was drinking his life away, and becoming more verbally abusive than ever. I will save you the gory details of the horror story that became my life. Instead, I'll take complete responsibility for it, "This is all because you didn't listen".

God seemed completely gone. Every time something bad happened, I thought it was punishment for not listening. I grew up in a strict Catholic home where I was taught that God's punishment followed when I didn't listen, or did "bad" things.

I remember arguing with my Grandmother in my parent's kitchen when I was about 8 years old. I was yelling at her, and I knew I was being disrespectful, so I ran out the back door and tripped on the way down the steps. Only a moment before, my Father had pulled into the driveway from work (I hadn't heard him with all the yelling that was happening) and was now standing over me. I looked up at him with tears rolling down my face while holding my bruised knee. "See that", he said, "God punished you for yelling at your Grandmother". He took me inside and made me apologize. The lesson that stuck with me that day wasn't "be respectful to my grandmother," it was "God punishes me when I do something wrong". So, in my mind, the abuse was punishment for not listening to God on my wedding day.

A Whisper of Encouragement

AL-Anon is for friends and families of alcoholics. I had been so beaten down emotionally and spiritually as well as physically, that I gratefully accepted an invitation to a meeting, hoping I would learn something that would help me, like how to turn back time so I could say "no" on that fateful day.

I took the steps one at a time. The first: "We admitted that we were powerless over alcohol and that our lives had become unmanageable". I knew my life was unmanageable. I seemed to have lost complete control of who I was. I didn't recognize myself in the mirror. My life was no longer my own. The second step is "Came to believe that a power greater than ourselves could restore us to sanity". How was I ever going to do this step? My relationship with God was all but dead because I didn't listen and was still being punished. Although it took a long time, and lots of searching, I was able to go from "Good Orderly Direction" to finally hearing the whispers of God again.

I remember the day I heard the first one. It was early in the morning after a long night. I was beyond distraught. He had found out I was going to meetings a few weeks before and had "forbid" me to attend again. I had tucked the daily reader I bought at the meeting into my dresser drawer. Because he "forbid" me to have anything to do with "those people" I was so afraid of being caught reading the book, that I kept it hidden.

On that particular morning, while I was sobbing and asking myself how my life had gotten to that point, I called out to God for help. I heard a whisper. It said "Open the book". At first I wasn't sure what that meant, and through the tears, I said, "what?" I heard it again, "Open the book". I looked around for a book, didn't see any. Then it hit me. I took the daily reader out of the drawer, and opened to a random page. I can't tell you what was on that page, or even what the topic was. Whatever it was, it gave me a sense of peace and comfort that I hadn't thought possible that morning. I knew I had to continue reading and get myself to meetings. I did whatever it took to get there. I went to as many meetings as I could. I struggled with the higher power thing, but was hopeful for the first time in a long time that my life could change.

I was still looking for answers to the questions I was asking about how to end the nightmare that had become my life. Then one day, on my way home from an early morning walk, I asked for a sign that God was still in my life. In the maple tree in front of my house, I spied a beautiful red cardinal. I knew that was my sign. How? Well the night before at the meeting, someone shared that they knew when God was near because they saw a red cardinal. Under my breath, I was saying, "Yeah, right!" That morning, when

I saw that Cardinal, I learned 2 things: Not to be judgmental, and that God is **ALWAYS** with me. When I saw that cardinal I actually heard a little giggle inside. I know it was the same whispered breath of God. He had been there all the time, I had to be ready to see Him and hear the whispers of His heart to mine again.

I learned many things about myself and about alcoholism and I will be forever grateful for the reconnection to God that I found in the steps and the safety of AL-Anon. When I saw that cardinal, I took the third step; "Made a decision to turn our will and our lives over to the care of God as we understood him."

A Whisper of Confidence

Though my husband wasn't changing, things were changing in my heart and in my life. God was whispering confidence into me. In the program, I was regaining my confidence. It was time to start taking control of and responsibility for my own life. I hadn't felt that while I was being victimized, but as my confidence grew, and in taking responsibility, I realized it wasn't just him abusing me, I was allowing myself to be abused.

Step 4 is "Made a searching and fearless moral inventory of our lives." I read it as, Made a searching and fearful inventory. I was still filled with fear, and was "acting as if" every day with hope that acting would become reality. I was hearing God whisper in my heart that I was on the right path; this was the way out of the nightmare I had been living. So, no matter how afraid I felt, I was writing my inventory, I knew that God had my back.

In my email, I get a daily "Note from the Universe." I call them "Love notes from God." They are always perfectly timed, like this one... "Teresa, fear just means you've forgotten how deeply you're loved, how safe you are, and that happiness will return, like you've never known it before."

I have come to discover this statement as truth. I am confident it's because I took the direction from God whispering in my heart.

It was time to find someone who I completely trusted to share my inventory with. Completely trusted? I didn't trust anyone! Step 5 is "Admitted to God, to ourselves and to another human being the exact nature of our wrongs." I finally had God in my life and I was listening to everything He was telling me in His whispers. I decided to trust my sponsor, who had also become a great friend. I disclosed everything, even things that I didn't think I would ever repeat because I was so full of shame and guilt.

In the process, it was suggested I speak to a particular local priest. He looked like any picture I've ever seen of Jesus; he even wore a robe and sandals. I felt like I was sitting before Jesus Himself when I walked into his office. I knew it was against the "laws of the church" to get a divorce but I wanted out of my marriage. I needed direction.

When I told him how I had been living, he advised me to get out alive while I still could! It was okay to get a divorce! I was elated and scared at the same time and I also heard the whisper of confidence I needed from God.

Step 6: "Were entirely ready to have God remove these defects of character". I was ready to have my inability to take direction and listen removed. Surrender wasn't easy for me. I wanted to have a say in everything. That was a huge defect of character. I was ready, and surrender is ongoing. Next, I was able to let go of things that kept me bound "Humbly asked Him to remove our shortcomings" is the 7th step. It takes humility to surrender. I remember asking God to take away the fear. Courage began to take its place. I learned that courage is fear that's said its prayers. I bring my fears to God, and they somehow morph into courage and courageous action.

I knew God had my back and I was willing to do what it took to move on. My courageous character was evolving; I was no longer stuck in fear and criticism. I was further along the path to free-dom from what still seemed like sanity to me.

Whispers of Direction

Once I got the "go ahead" from the priest, I called a lawyer. During this time, several things happened that warranted me get-ting orders of protection from the court. He was still very active in his addition and at this time, my son was in the first grade.

The next time my husband raised his hand to me, I decided I was DONE with abuse, and engaged the help of my Al-Anon friends to keep me and my son safe. That afternoon, I moved in with a good friend. We hid my car in her garage, and the following morn-ing I went to court in pursuit of an order of protection for us. Sometimes there are law students in the court to help.

I told the young lady what I wanted the judge to order. I wanted my husband to stop hitting me, I wanted him to get coun-seling, and I wanted him to not be able to pick up my son from school. You see, God was whispering to me that if I didn't do that, there was great potential for danger to my son; my husband could pick him up at the school and run with him. I made it clear to my new 'helper' what I was asking for. She didn't think that the judge would honor the last part.

When it came time for me to stand before the judge, though I was afraid, all the fear ran from me when the law student was addressing the judge. She didn't mention that part about not pick-ing my son up from school! I was determined. So, I addressed the judge. I don't remember the exact words; I am sure they came from God. I do know I asked for what I wanted, because my husband was taking pain killers as well as drinking. Many times, I could see the evidence of it in his eyes, but to someone, like the clerk at the counter in the school, who was unfamiliar with this, there may be no reason for her not to release my son to this man, putting him in danger.

The judge agreed and gave me the order. I had purposely kept my son home from school that day while I was at court. With papers in hand, I went to the school, had a conversation with the principal and brought her up to speed on what was happening. She agreed that she would do everything she could to keep my son safe.

The very next day, my husband went to the school to pick my son up. When they refused to let him take the child, he went around the side of the building where my son's classroom was and attempted to kidnap him from the classroom. Thankfully the teacher was alerted, and called the principal who made sure that the attempt to take my child would not happen again without police intervention. For now, we were safe.

Eventually, I had to go home so my friends could have their privacy back. I engaged the help of an intervention counselor who helped get my husband into treatment so I could go home without fear. Thankfully, it went well, and he entered treatment. My son and I moved back home.

Step 8 is "Make a list of all persons we had harmed, and became willing to make amends to them all." This was tough for me, because the way I saw it, I was the one who was being harmed. I was the first person to put on that list. My son was second, my friends who had been put in harm's way having helped me to be safe more than once, were added. The list grew to many people, including my husband. Why? Well, my actions before I sought help in AL-Anon were feeding his disease. When I think of the insanity, it still chills me to the bone.

I would have to act on this list with Step 9: "Made direct amends to such people wherever possible, except when to do so would injure them or others." People who were on my list who I hadn't seen in years showed up at the time I was actively doing this step! It still amazes me how they were there to hear my amends, and then were gone as quickly as they had shown up. Personally, I think it was all Divine intervention. I even recently made amends to my now ex-husband. Although many years have passed, I'm still forgiving myself for the things I'd exposed my son to. I trust this unforgiveness will pass too. I do what I can to take care of myself and when I need help, I ask friends for support. I am no longer alone. I have God holding me up and friends watching my back and lifting my spirits.

Steps 10, 11 and 12 are commonly called 'maintenance steps' Step 10: "Continued to take personal inventory and when we were wrong promptly admitted it." Step 11: "Sought through prayer and meditation to improve our conscious contact with God, as we understood Him, praying only for knowledge of His will for us and the power to carry that out." And finally, Step 12: "Having has a spiritual awakening as the result of these steps; we tried to carry this message to alcoholics and to practice these principles in all out affairs." I can honestly say that these last 3 steps keep me in relationship with God and able to hear the whispers that come in my quiet time with Him. These steps are not just for alcoholics. They have been adapted in many ways to help people with all kinds of addictions, including addictions to other people. I was addicted to my alcoholic husband.

Over the years I have moved far away from my ex-husband, begun a new life that includes making pottery, a gift that had been asleep for many years. I have developed relationships with people all over the world, and I write daily. I feel called to share what I have experienced. Sometimes it's difficult to go back to that place of hurt and insanity, but I always come away from it with gratitude. I'm so grateful that I've learned to listen to the whispers and follow through on the little 'nudges' God gives me. I've become an active part of a wonderful church and have put God at the center of all that I do.

As I reflect on this writing, I am filled with gratitude for the steps that I took to get where I am today. I am a coach, a speaker, an author in a bestselling book series, and I'm a potter. I use the art of making pottery as an illustration for transformation in my coaching. Each of us begins as a ball of clay and we are transformed throughout our lives to beautiful works of art!

The 12 steps saved my life. I have transformed through them. Here they are rewritten from my new perspective:

1. I am Powerful
2. The greater good for all would be realizing the steps I need to take for me and that God can help me along the way, if I let him.
3. I came to the realization that I do not walk alone. God is always with me. I let him guide me.
4. When I searched within myself, I realized that my outer world did not reflect my inner world.
5. I came to the realization that there are no true wrongs. Everything happens for my benefit and through this realization I am able to take my power back.
6. By letting go of some of the things that were clearly holding me back, I developed courage to redirect my life. I developed a courageous character rather than one that was afraid and critical.
7. I surrendered my weaknesses and moved in the direction of opportunity rather than obstacles in my ongoing journey.
8. I forgave myself and in doing so, made room to forgive others and for them to forgive me.
9. Take every opportunity to make right the things I may have felt were wrong by making amends as I feel led to.
10. Take personal responsibility. I always check in with God to make sure I haven't 'checked out'.

11. From this day forward, I pray the prayers that are faith backed and not fear based, knowing that God's goodness is abundant.
12. My spirit is alive and joyful. What good is it for me to know something and not share it?

I encourage you to listen to those whispers; they are powerful words of guidance and purpose. May your life's journey be joyful and abundantly blessed!

About the Author

Teresa Velardi is a leader, author, speaker, publisher and host of Transformational Tuesdays. Living her life in authenticity and gratitude, while making a difference in the lives of others are Teresa's passion and purpose. Knowing that everyone has a story to tell, she is also committed to helping people to share their stories with the world.

As the host of Transformational Tuesdays, Teresa often says that the one thing in life that is constant is change. We are forever changing and growing into the awesome people we were created to be. Also a skilled potter, Teresa often uses the art of making pottery as an illustration for transformation.

To learn more or connect with Teresa go to www.teresavelardi.com.

To register for Transformational Tuesdays and receive a free gift go to www.transformationaltuesdays.com.

For more on sharing your story in an upcoming book, go to www.yourstorymattersnow.com.

"As you continue your "purpose" journey, journal, journal, journal. Remember to journal daily! Both your words and writing contain power!"

C. Denise

Chapter 5

The Purpose Principle
Dr. C. Denise Richardson

I dedicate this chapter to my mother, Nancy M. Burton, for who she is, was, and is to be! God has used you to make me better! Always, C. Denise

"The purpose of life is to live it, to taste experience to the utmost, to reach out eagerly and without fear for newer and richer experience." - Eleanor Roosevelt

There must be more to [my] life than this. I tell myself this to maintain what little sanity I have left. I realize that this mediocre life is NOT God's best life for me. Here we are out searching for homeless people to share the gospel of Christ with and she's calling my phone incessantly. This is when I initially began to realize that I was unfulfilled. I had a husband who loved and respected me unconditionally. Unlike the beautiful "Bey", I was flawed, marred, and scarred. But I had one thing going for me. I had truly been born again! My desire after a decade of marriage was to serve the underserved, the neglected and misunderstood. I wanted to become more involved in our communities. You see, meeting with the same folks..."family" on the same day annually had become sort of monotonous and unfulfilling. I don't even think my husband fully comprehended my longing to be outside with those whom I deemed less fortunate. He obliged, nonetheless. I told you, he's my biggest supporter. And, he loved me unconditionally. The phone rings again. This time, it's our eldest daughter calling to find out where I am because my mom is tired of waiting for me. They're prepared to bless the food so they can eat.

She's expecting me to say nothing about her current, makeshift relationship with "him"! "Did you speak to "Johnny" she inquires. This is yet another reason I'd begun to loathe these "family" gatherings. "I'm grown and don't feel like this stupid crap" is what I'm thinking! However, I respond in the respectful manner that is expected of me, "Yes, I spoke." "**LEAVE ME ALONE!** That mane (I didn't see him as a "man" but as a "mane" speaking in my hood vernacular) is married...with grown kids and I'm **NOT** one of 'em!" Yes, this was one of the major reasons I loathed visiting my mother's home. I don't require an etiquette refresher course. Good Lord. I am a Christian and, I will always conduct myself as such. I want to share with you how easy it can be-come to attempt to be someone you truly are not, and how purpose can be stifled if we seek to please people rather than God. I loved my mom. However, these experiences were becoming my real life "thorn in the flesh".

Situations similar to the above referenced scenario occurred frequently and, I wasn't a very sociable woman when I was forced to repudiate my [spiritual] convictions. The blatant dis-regard for my feelings because I was "her" child made absolutely no sense [to me]. These experiences always left me a little less happy, a little more angry and a lot more intentional about my purpose! Holidays, birthdays, and other social gatherings challenged me to step out of my com-fort zone to be who I'd long ago professed to be.

Purpose not only illuminates my tempestuous experiences but "it" also reveals the reason my purpose either captivates or repels broken women! I realize that my passionate, no nonsense attitude may come off as condescending. However, that's truly not my heart. I'm empathetic to the myriad of mountains women have experienced. Consequently, I invest in the education, social, financial, and spiritual development of hurting women. Because I am a survivor of both physical and sexual abuses, survivors of physical and sexual abuse truly own my heart in direct connection to purpose. Often times, women aren't receptive to challenge, chastisement or change. I know. I, similar to you, have found myself unwilling to transform. It was only when I'd hit rock bottom that I'd be willing to own my own mistakes and choices without blaming others. Challenge, chastisement (through God's word), and change are prerequisites for purpose activation and continuation.

I remember the first opportunity I had to share the testimony of a woman who had been sexually abused numerous times during her childhood. I also remember the horrified looks on the faces of those I was training. Some were visibly uncomfortable, others appeared incensed while others appeared strangely aloof. I continued sharing the young woman's testimony of poor decision making whichever ultimately led to her dysfunctional, physically abusive relationship with a guy two years older than she. This piece of information seemed to agitate more of the men than women. However, when I began to share how this woman decided (at the age of twenty-three began) to change her life by making better choices in [her] relationships, education and spiritual life; the sheer astonishment in the eyes of all the participants spoke volumes! I don't know if it was the fact that this woman had beaten most of the odds or the fact that she was no longer a general "statistic" had caused such astonishment! Then, I pondered the fact that this woman had managed to earn four degrees while raising a family, working and engaging in community activism. Then again, maybe it was the element of surprise! I revealed that I, Dr. C. Denise, and this mysterious woman were one in the same!

It's an amazing yet overwhelming experience to share with the world my [personal] journey. The ups and downs. The joys and pains of surviving various abuses while finding inner courage to inspire others! This is what I term "The Purpose Principle". When you find inspiration to encourage others even during the tumultuous experiences of your life, you have already begun the purpose continuum. The trajectory that purpose journeys isn't always the most ideal; however, it will certainly demonstrate God's authority and the individual's commitment to "her".

The purpose principle is that "thing" that drives you to inspire others to define, recognize and inspire purpose in oneself and in others! The "purpose" component establishes the fundamentals of the passion for the purpose! The "principle" is that component that is most important to your "why"! The "principle" is the conduit to activating the "purpose"! Wow! It's that "thing" that pushes you to strive for more, for greater, for excellence!

The women who can't seem to support [other] women have likely been damaged emotionally, physically, psychologically or sexually. There's an element of humanity that interferes with her ability to see the greatness within her sister. The greatness within your sister should resonate purpose, passion, power and eventually prosperity. When a woman of purpose passionately pursues [her] purpose no matter what she is presently enduring; she can shake and awaken purpose in anyone...including her harshest critics! The "purpose principle" defies logic! It defies human reasoning to the degree that purpose can quite possibly be the most inspirational factor in an individual's life! Purpose offers motivation and inspiration. Purpose propels those who thrive on pleasing God by inspiring others to action. And, action reveals the faith component. The "purpose principle" always overrides fear, intimidation, procrastination, or limitations. Because the call to greatness requires one to adapt to various scenarios and circumstances, a committed call to one's own purpose principle is vitally important to the overall vision within the purpose.

> *"I am convinced that the jealous, the angry, the bitter and the egotistical are the first to race to the top of mountains. A confident person enjoys the journey, the people they meet along the way and sees life not as a competition. They reach the summit last because they know God isn't at the top waiting for them. He is down below helping his followers to understand that the view is glorious where ever you stand." -Shannon L. Alder*

> *"I wish to have a heart and mind that is free so I can dance forever." Paula Geeter*

A purpose without vision is like an organization without a mission statement. In order to effectively operate in purpose, consistency and disciplined determination are integral components to fulfilling the "purpose" mandate. Purpose isn't simply what you do, it's "who" you are! The passion behind the purpose principle defines my purpose niche. The "purpose principle" is undeniably one of the most rewarding principles known to mankind! If not acknowledged, it can be one of the most self defeating principles known to mankind.

> *"Forget about the fast lane. If you really want to fly, just harness your power to your passion." - Oprah Winfrey*

Purpose is "who" I am. Purpose is "who" you are! Purpose is the reason you've elected to purchase and read this anthology. Purpose is the passion of the principle to do what you do without much, if any, effort. Everything and every person has an intended purpose or purposes. The "purpose principle" answers a very important question and, very often it authenticates and validates you as a woman of purpose while simultaneously inspiring [other] women of purpose. Authentication and validation are revealed when you own your purpose unapologetically. Authentication and validation is **NOT** pleasing individuals or seeking others' approval. Are you alright shaking purpose [in others] when everyone in your circle is not a cheerleader for you? A significant number and women seek the validation of their peers when purpose does that alone if we live a life rich in purpose. Say this, "I personify Purpose!" I am purpose personified! Purpose is what I enjoy doing that is both practical and natural to the comprehensive trajectory toward destiny!

Women "**RICH**" in purpose exude confidence and boldness in the face of adversity! We take purpose by the "horns" and ride it to completion. He who has begun a good work in you will perform it until the day of Jesus Christ. The "purpose" is perfected through the works we do in the earth. Everyone will not "get it". But those who do will likely never forget the day that purpose was awakened and shaken within them. Plan each day to shake purpose in someone. It's such a rewarding experience to know that you have undoubtedly won a soul to Christ. I say won a soul because God is the author of purpose. He is the One who instills the purpose. By shaking purpose God will no doubt begin to stir the gift(s).

"Be a woman who commands purpose to awaken daily." - C. Denise

---

Who am I called to serve?

It's imperative that every woman of purpose asks this question concerning her individual purpose(s). If we neglect to ask this vitally important question, we may very well find ourselves overworked, overstretched, and under-appreciated. No one likes to feel unappreciated. Conversely, the purpose minded woman does not seek accolades for living her life purposefully. But rather, she lives her life passionately and unapologetically in direct relation to her mandate, her call her purpose.

Today is Monday and I'm shouting at the girls, "Rise and shine, give God the glory." I knew instinctively that three of the four girls would shift gears and progress through their various morning routines. All would comply except the eldest. So, it's funny because years earlier I'd attended a unique spiritual training for entrepreneurs hosted by Al and Hattie Hollingsworth on "birthing dreams" through faith. I also walked away with a unique cd that included a countdown to assist with time management which, by the way, is a weakness for me. I enjoyed using the audio in the mornings to activate purpose while disciplining the lack of time management in our morning family routine. Serving those in your family can be a true dichotomy, because while developing purpose is truly rewarding; it is unapologetically draining also! Don't neglect the purpose. It's the principle thing.

The "purpose principle" also identifies those whom you've been called to serve. I'm called to serve people. And, because my specific call is directly linked to women and children; I can identify with the struggle to comprehend individual purpose. "Who" is your Jane Doe? When was the last time you "served" her? Are you connecting with or contacting "Janes" consistently?

What does [my] purpose resemble? Although there are general similarities, each woman's purpose is as unique as the DNA within us. My purpose resembles me! My characteristics, my passions, my disciplined determination comprises and defines my destiny and so does yours.

Purpose Principle Continuum

The "purpose principle" requires us to intentionally seek out and pursue purpose. Every woman's purpose is unique to God's specific plans for her life! Invariably, purpose driven women require purpose driven connections. This is in no way an attack on or indict ment against women who are seeking their way and have yet to tap into their "purposes". The connections women make with other women of purpose are crucial to the continual development of both individual and collective purpose. I call these connections "purpose squads". Selecting a "purpose squad" requires prayer and wisdom. A purpose squad includes other women of purpose who will hold you accountable to your purpose while encouraging you to trust the process! Also, your next steps include research, research, research. Ask yourself, "Is my purpose truly beneficial to others?" "Is my purpose enriching the lives of those whom I reach?" Many women have traded their "purpose" mantles for imitation mantles. We all have either very productive, busy or idle lives. Productive lives yield fruit of purpose in others while busy lives yield tainted purpose in others. Idle lives yield strife and regret. A "purpose" life commands liberty to activate purpose in others. Interruptions may temporarily impede the process but, authentic purpose can't be stopped by outside factors! Life happens! That's a fact! We mustn't allow family, career, life's circumstances, or surprises to distract us for prolonged periods of time. When we do, we become stagnant, bitter, angry, envious, and resentful. If you are experiencing a season of stagnation or anxiety, you may need to **#RICH** (Reinstate your purpose, Inspire your passion, Change your circles, & Have faith in your God). Let's shake purpose in women across the nations! We are international purpose shakers!

The women who share their struggles and promote God's strength in this anthology are the kinds of women who consistently transform lives in the lives of those connected to them! Purpose transformation requires challenge. And, often times significant numbers of women.

Tina, your passion to insightfully see purpose in all women reveals a significant principle many conveniently forget...to possess the mind of Christ. When we possess the mind of Christ, our thoughts are at the peak of highest purpose potential! Philippians chapter 2 verse 5 challenges us to "let this mind be in you, which was also in Christ Jesus". Jesus lived a life of purpose continually. Although He experienced opposition, He never abandoned [His] purpose.

Chiquita, the one hour principle has the potential to shake the purpose of all people no matter their gender or race! You are one passionate purpose advocate! The world should be so blessed to meet someone like Chiquita. Strategically Engineering Purpose.

Cynthia, you are the people's purpose promoter! Your unique manner of speaking life to that which many consider "dead" reveals your authentic love and appreciation for families of great destiny who, should they ever decide to accept the mantle offered to them, are destined for even greater! The Aftermath Produces Purpose.

Onika, the lady who has faced her [own] self-esteem demons to walk in purpose while inviting other women to live a full life of purpose without regret! The boldness you possess requires only an authentic awareness of who one really is according to the word of God. Continue building confidence through identified purpose. Purpose looks great on you! Confidently Purposed.

Genia, how blessed are the girls and women whom you inspire! Communities are forever transformed because you've taken a stand against mediocrity and complacency while standing up for individuality and purpose in the lives of women from all races and backgrounds! Continue empowering women with God's truth and purpose! Purpose forerunner.

Teresa, you are definitely a "purpose agent!" Your ability to connect women of various back-grounds demonstrates your authentic love for us! As you humbly challenge women to accept transformation, you also challenge us to divinely seek purpose within ourselves! Transformational Purpose Agent.

About the Author

Dr. C Denise Richardson, women's and children's abuse prevention proponent, humanitarian, community leader, freelance writer, author, Life Strategist, ordained minister, former public school educator, administrator and Ex. Director of CDR Unlimited, is a survivor of both child sexual abuse (CSA) and domestic violence (DV). C. Denise inspires women to confront personal and professional mountains in order to transform into women of prayer, power, purpose and prosperity! These four pillars correlate to individual and corporate legacies! C. Denise inspires women to activate/awaken purpose first in themselves and then others! #MountainMovers and #PurposeShakers are her most notable conferences. Dr. C. also offers monthly MastHERmind sessions for the aforementioned conference titles. Dr. C. loves women and is a radical catalyst for life, love, & legacy through accountability, faith, application, & collaboration!

C. Denise earned four degrees that include one undergrad, two masters, & one doctoral degree. Additionally, C. Denise enrolls in CEUs in education, psychology, and counseling courses annually. Her commendations include community activism with the homeless, socially disadvantaged, and abused. C. Denise is also a member of various, notable community organizations.

C. Denise, like many of her followers, has endured challenges, setbacks, and betrayals. However, she's also experienced triumphs, joys, and accomplishments. Dr. C. sis obsessed with seeing women encourage, support, and empower other women! It's her absolute favorite! She believes the world needs more of it! Because she is so passionate about women, she continues to offer life changing, mind altering courses that both challenge and support women's empowerment!

Dr. C. recognizes the significance of authenticity and accessibility! She acknowledges that she is no different than other women EXCEPT she opened the door to opportunity and that she has shared and continues to share her CSA and domestic abuse experiences unapologetically and unashamedly! She is passionate about her role in the lives of women! C. Denise partners with other women from various backgrounds, races, socioeconomic statuses, religions, & nationalities for the greater good of our world!

Dr. C. is married to Cedric Richardson (19 years) and, they work together in ministry, community, business, and family. They oversee both Life Changers Outreach Ministries Corporation (LCOMC), a 501(c)3 organization and Life Changers Church International (LCCI) in Memphis, TN. The central objective of this faith based ministry is to restore and reconcile families to Christ through the word of God. We do this through a number of methods including, but not limited to mentorship, individual and family counseling, life skill planning, literacy education, and computer and technology training. Three of their six daughters serve in various capacities of the aforementioned outreach.

www.cdrunlimited.com
C Denise Richardson: FB
@DrCDenise:Twitter & Instagram
richstrategist@gmail.com

"The excitement you feel in both your heart and belly...that's purpose! Grab her and NEVER let her go!"

C. Denise

Chapter 6

Purpose Driven, No Matter What!
Onika Shirley

Physical and mental abuse exposed my purpose. I am a survivor of sexual abuse. My struggles, my story and my emotional thinking revealed to me my purpose. The woman I am today reveals that I am purpose driven no matter what! Purpose Shakers will be challenged. I have learned that just because purpose is discovered and you are committed to living within your purpose it does not exonerate you from adversities of this world. In fact, "purpose shakers" attract more challenges and opposition than we repel, the more purposeful we appear to be. Through my own hurts, mistakes and tragedies I have decided to shake purpose in others. God told me that this life is not my own and that I was created with a purpose. He has given me the directions, He allowed the life experiences, and He gave me a spirit of power, strength and equipped me with a sound mind. I had to let go and let God because there's no peace or joy in a situation that God's grace is no longer a part of. Everything I experienced in my past has served a purpose. My struggles, my survival, my tragedies and my ability to conquer the odds against me brought me here. I am here to serve others.

God gives us time to heal and in being healed personally, I am free to share my experiences with you. I will show you that God is powerful and not emotional. God really is concerned about his people. Through Him caring for me I discovered that my power and purpose is in front of me and not behind me. I share my experiences just to encourage and inspire you and to show you that life can go on after you have been hurt or when you have experienced failure. I had to declare and decree that enough was enough in my life because I had allowed the enemy to hold me hostage in my mind for a long time. That hold remained strong until one day I said "Lord, I forgive him." In forgiving my aggressor, I started to experience peace. I learned that the Holy Spirit is a gentleman. He is polite and He will not force you to do anything, but He is a wonderful "helper" if you will allow him to help you.

Life for me as a little girl was challenging, but God never left my side or my heart. His word tells me that "He will never leave nor forsake me." I started to believe that He was there all the time. He didn't allow the enemy to kill me nor take my hope away. God called my earthly father home at an early age. I was only 9 years old when he called him home. I was not in the home with him so I never really had the opportunity to establish a relationship with him. I never questioned God about it because, at age 9, I really didn't understand what his death meant and at the time it didn't have much impact on me. I have since regretted not having my dad, but I managed to survive because God showed me that He still has a purpose for my life and it was not about my happiness but all about my holiness and the glory of God.

Not even a year later, at the innocent age of 10, I was sexually assaulted. Many people have been robbed of the life God destined for them because of self-punishment, guilt and shame. Sexual abuse, rape, assault, and incest are not the victim's fault and we shouldn't allow anyone to influence our thinking to believe it was our fault or that there are reasons to justify it. No one in their right mind purposely designs destruction, hurt, and pain in their life. I couldn't be brought to believe this way. I was made to feel shame and guilt, but God gave me strength and wisdom to see things from a different perspective. "Nothing just happens!"

I am a survivor of sexual abuse. I faced this unwanted, undeserved, and unwarranted experience as a child. I was on a public school field trip with adult chaperones. This violation of my body and my mind was the evidence of how unsafe I really was in the presence of these people. Parents don't send their children to school or on a school field trip with what happened to me in mind. School field trips can be exciting experiences for both students and teachers alike. Field trips are an opportunity for young students to get out of the boundaries of the classroom and use their child wonders and senses to explore a live lesson or interactive concept. Successful field trips take thoughtful planning and great people. It is vital to choose chaperones carefully before allowing them to accompany students on a fieldtrip. Predators will invest the time and sometimes the money to exploit others.

I was on a school field trip to Hot Springs, AR. Funny that I can't remember my excitement so well as I remember what happened in place of fun filled events. I was sexually violated by one of the teachers of the district there as a chaperone. How could this happen? Why did this happen? Afterward, I wanted only for the memories to be cleared, and I wanted to just go back to being the child that I was before it all happened. I know sexual violation recovery is possible because I did it, but it takes times and it takes effort.

At such a young age, I was devastated on the inside. I was embarrassed. I remember going to counseling in Marianna, AR and how much I hated it. I didn't like having to talk about it, and I didn't want to think about it. This thing made me bitter and it impacted my grades because my thoughts about education were clouded due to an educator being such a sick person. I was a honor roll student, but the replays of that night, that day, and that time clouded my head space so I decided to act out to avoid thinking about it. I didn't want an educator to tell me anything!

I had to learn to love and care for myself after this traumatic event. It may not have been anything to the world, but it was something to me. I was the one who was afraid. I was the one who was violated. I was the one who was truly impacted. I conquered the thing that was initially blocking my educational success. I had to condition my mind to intentionally block the memories, the newspaper articles and the lies being aired over the radio. This thing could never be changed, but it could be managed. Pain doesn't just go away by denying its existence. You will do one of three things. A person will ignore it and it will resurrect itself in a mid-life crisis, you will numb it and keep it a secret and it will eat you up on the inside, or you will deny it and get really super religious about it.

I had a barrier up for a very long time. I stayed to myself and made a lot of bad decisions. I had a lot of bad thoughts towards the individuals that were responsible for hurting me, but Jesus started showing me in the middle of my pain and at the threshold of my disappointments that Luke 7:21 and James 1:2 were still encouraging words from The Lord. God said in your anger don't sin, but he gave me permission to feel. God told me to give him everything I was feeling. He wanted me to give him everything I had. Jesus then reminded me that He suffered for me to live so I was able to bond with Jesus like never before. He told me to have grace for myself and once I started having grace for myself, I was able to have grace for others. It is okay to tell The Lord how you feel. Some pain can hurt so badly, but I have never blamed God because I know God sent Jesus as my redeemer. He showed me that heart and heads wounds can be healed and the pain can go away. We are guilty of trying to cover our pain with so many different things verses healing our pain with our Lord and Savior Jesus Christ.

At the age of 16, I became a teenage mother. I was looking for love in all the wrong places. I was covering up my pain. I found out I was 3 months pregnant during my 10th grade school year. It was a very difficult situation. There were many decisions that needed to be made concerning my baby. I had to decide what was best for me and my child, so I promised myself that no matter what I would not drop out of school and I had to get a job. I got my own place at the age of 16. The baby's father wasn't in the picture. I still knew despite all that had happened, purpose still had to be shaken.

I made a choice to stick it out. It was hard sometimes, especially when my little baby girl wanted to play in the middle of the night and just hours before time for me to get up for school. I had to fix the wrong, make the sacrifice, and get the work done. I enrolled in the home-bound study program while on maternity leave because I was determined to graduate. I completed the 10th grade and we were doing fine. At the start of my 11th grade year, I got my first job working at Sonic Drive-In as a line cook. I went to school in the day time and worked at night. I worked from 5pm to 11pm during the week and 5pm to 1am on the weekends. I worked, hired a babysitter and went to school every day.

I spoke to the adversities I was facing. I was blessed to get through school, I finished what I started and my dreams became my reality. Many adversities I faced, but they were spoken to and they were moved. God showed me and He continues to reveal to me that there's a purpose in my being here and that He is not through with me yet! I know and understand that I have purpose in this world and I am shaking purpose every day. My purpose is to let my light shine and to encourage someone to keep pressing past the adversities they may face. God helped me to stop giving the enemy access to my life, in my mind and in my heart. Today, I am able to help encourage, motivate, and inspire others. Through my pain, I birthed Action Speaks Volume where I help others build unshakable confidence, learn how to be alone but not lonely, and to value their uniqueness.

Each of us is created with a purpose. We are each in possession of any number of unique gifts and talents but none of them are for the glory of the receiver, but they are given for the glory of God. We sometimes experience unfavorable situations in our lives, but we are heirs of a God that gives us a second chance at life no matter what has happened to us and without regard for what we have done. God can give us what we need in order to begin the healing process, and he gives us permission to forgive and to be forgiven for all our shortcomings. God has created each of us uniquely and with reason; his reason is for His divine purpose. I am shaking purpose because despite the things that I have experienced in my life I have discovered, developed and deployed energy into God's purpose for me.

When life is simply viewed from the outside, onlookers seem to think that you have it going on and that your life is problem free. I am an example of life not being problem free, but with God I have been given the strength to overcome and conquer the things and people in my life that try to destroy me. I know there is a purpose for my life and that's why I am willing to do God's will. I am committed to being a conduit for God. He sends His power through me freely because I am submitted and I'm a surrendered vessel to Him daily. I am willing to do what He tells me to do, I am willing to go wherever He will have me to go, and I am willing to say whatever He will have me say.

The Lord has reminded me that if it weren't for my past experiences, struggles, tragedies, hurts, and disappointments I wouldn't be here now. I serve those who can't help themselves and I'm reaching out to those who have a desire to help themselves. My pain turned into my purpose which is now my passion. "Speak up for those who cannot speak for themselves; ensure justice for those being crushed. Yes, speak up for the poor and helpless, and see that they get justice. Proverbs 31:8-9. Life is valuable and purpose is divine. God loves me and He shows that He cares. I thank God for keeping me and I thank God for helping me. Once I learned to love myself I was able to love others. My life story helped me discover my purpose and your story will help you discover your purpose. Your purpose will reveal to you that you make a difference! Purpose seeker, it's time to discover and act in your purpose!

About the Author

Onika Shirley is an accomplished professional who leads from a position in senior management in manufacturing. She achieved the Dean's List every semester while pursuing her MBA and graduated Magna Cum Laude while earning her Bachelor's in Business Accounting. The 4-year former President of the Greater Memphis chapter of the National Association of Professional Women authored **Women We Must Stand Strong**. She was featured as part of the cover story for Ordinary People, Spring 2012. She was also sought out by the Phillips County Community College to instruct The Manufacturing Enterprise during the Fall semester 2015. Of all of her achievements, she is most proud of her profound faith in Christ as her personal Lord and Savior.

Onika proves her selfless dedication to helping others by serving as a foster parent as well as an adoptive parent. Onika has not reached this level of success without having to overcome much adversity. The adversities she faced has given her strength, motivation, and the resiliency to become the Life Clarity and Action Coach that she is today. She helps others build unshakable confidence. Today, she blogs about being relevant and other experiences at the Huffington Post.

Onika Shirley, MBA
Life Clarity and Action Coach
Founder/CEO
Action Speaks Volume
Helena-West Helena, AR 72390
Phone: 901-264-0761
actionspeaksvolume@gmail.com
http://actionspeaksvolum.com

"Purpose is the drum major for destiny! Allow "her" to lead you to higher heights toward destiny."

C. Denise

Chapter 7

Listening with Purpose
Teresa Velardi

Call to me and I will answer you and tell you great and unsearchable things you do not know. - Jeremiah 33:3

Did you hear that? Shhhhh...listen...did you hear that?

I can almost hear the sound of the leaves falling from the trees if I pay attention to them, can you?

Just before I fall asleep at night I can hear my heart beating in my chest, and my breathing slow down just before I slip into the world of slumber, can you?

When I pay attention, I can even hear the voice of God deep inside my spirit. The key is...I have to pay attention. Scripture tells me that God will answer me when I call to him, and I have called so many times. The reason that I don't hear the answers he gives me is because I'm too busy trying to figure out the answers to whatever I am asking in my own head. I've been drowning out the voice of God with all the chatter I make up in my mind about everything. At least that's how it used to be....I've learned to listen for the answers.

If you have children, I'm sure you can relate to the endless string of questions that little kids ask. One right after the other, they are like individual droplets of water to begin with, and then somehow they cluster up into a full bucket of water that seems like it can almost drown you. In the meantime, as the parent, we have the answers to many of the questions, but they will never get through the onslaught.

I think that's how many of us are when we ask for help, or for an answer from God. We keep rephrasing the question or asking a group of questions, and in the asking, we forget to listen for the answers. We get overwhelmed by our own thinking, or we get frustrated and emotional, not unlike our children and we drown God out. I believe that's why God sometimes brings people into our lives who can deliver His answers. We won't get still enough to listen to His voice within us, so He runs interference with people who somehow just seem to show up at the right time with the right words or the right stuff. Have you ever noticed that?

We are taught that God wants us to have a relationship with Him, so it's only logical that we will have to do some listening. Think about what it takes to build relationships with anyone. The first thing is conversation, which is defined as *the informal exchange of ideas by spoken words.* Someone talks and the other person listens and vice versa. Most of the time, if a relationship is lopsided, meaning one person is always dominating the conversation, the other person can tend to shut down or even leave the relationship because they can't be heard.

I'm not suggesting that God will leave if you don't listen, although there was a time in my life when I believed He did just that. When I was at the altar ready to be married, I heard God tell me not to do it. Not once, but twice in a matter of minutes. "Teresa, don't do this, I have something so much better for you." When I entered into the marriage anyway, I felt my heart sink. I felt like God had walked away, but it was me who abandoned myself and blocked my heart from hearing God. Maybe it was out of shame or guilt, but I cut myself off from being able to hear his voice...I would even say that I turned my back on God in that moment. I was miserable for a long time after that, both in my marriage and with myself.

Where in your life have you turned your back on yourself? Or on God even? He is always and in many ways, inviting us into relationship with Him. There was a church in the town where I grew up that had a sign out front and each week there would be a new message, scripture or quote put up. I'll always remember this one: *If God seems far away, who do you think moved?* Anytime I'm feeling disconnected from God, or from anyone else, I have to ask myself that question.

Listening with purpose is something we should do in every relationship or situation. I get frustrated with people who are always thinking about what they are going to say next instead of being fully present in the conversation with another person. I've had lots of practice with this throughout my life, and I get to use what I have learned every week on my Transformational Tuesdays show. If I'm not fully present in the conversation with my guest or my audience, the show is terrible. I've had situations where the guests have been halfheartedly paying attention, but that's not my issue. If I'm committed to taking one hundred percent responsibility for my life, then I am responsible for ALL areas of my life, one hundred percent of the time. Ok, so there are areas I'm still working on.

Let's look at some of the reasons to listen with purpose in day to day life. I'm sure when we master the art of listening to others; we will be able to listen to ourselves, and to the voice of God.

Listening for the purpose of:

- Being polite. It's rude to interrupt or to walk away when someone is speaking to you.
- Learning and Information. Listening is one of several ways that people learn and gather information. Listening (Auditory), Reading or watching (Visual) and through Touch (Kinesthetic) are the 3 main ways. How do you learn best?
- Bringing value to the other person. When we listen to someone speak, it shows we value their opinion or the information they are sharing.
- Building Trust. When we hold space for someone to share their heart or personal information about their life with us, it brings a level of trust to the relationship.
- Credibility. 1.) This goes along with building trust. When I say I'm holding what someone is telling me in confidence, I will never repeat it. That's the truth. The person whose secret I hold trusts me, and I am credible or trustworthy to that person as long as I hold what they have told me in confidence. 2.) I have done my research, and what I am telling you is the truth.
- Comprehension. Listening to understand.
- Decision making. Getting the facts will help you to decide what to buy, where to go, what to do. Listen, and ask questions to get answers you need to make the right choice for you.
- Enhanced cooperation. When you know what is expected of you, things just go more smoothly. Listen for direction.

All of these purposes for listening are evident in the relationships we have and in day to day living. They are also evident in my relationship with God, who I have learned to listen carefully.

Setting aside quiet time each day for the purpose of spending time with God and giving thanks for all that I have through him is mandatory for me. Yes, I miss some days, I am not perfect. I do notice a difference in how I feel and in how my day goes if I miss that time with Him.

I've heard myself say many times that we give to others from the overflow, and that we need to fill up our own cup before we can pour into others. So, I fill myself in the morning with gratitude and His word. What is the source of your time of filling up? Whatever it is, it will indeed lend itself to your being able to listen with purpose.

About the Author

Teresa Velardi is a leader, author, speaker, publisher and host of Transformational Tuesdays. Living her life in authenticity and gratitude, while making a difference in the lives of others are Teresa's passion and purpose. Knowing that everyone has a story to tell, she is also committed to helping people to share their stories with the world.

As the host of Transformational Tuesdays, Teresa often says that the one thing in life that is constant is change. We are forever changing and growing into the awesome people we were created to be. Also a skilled potter, Teresa often uses the art of making pottery as an illustration for transformation.

To learn more or connect with Teresa go to www.teresavelardi.com.

To register for Transformational Tuesdays and receive a free gift go to www.transformationaltuesdays.com.

For more on sharing your story in an upcoming book, go to www.yourstorymattersnow.com.

"Remember, prayer is communication, praise is adoration and purpose is elevation! Are you RICHly balanced in all three? Celebrate purpose every day! Remember your "why"!

C. Denise

Chapter 8

Released: Surviving an Alcholic Parent
Cynthia Snyder

"I have to go home." It's 2:00 in the morning; my husband and I had fallen asleep on the floor, which was not unusual when we relaxed to read or watch TV after a busy day at work. Why did I feel this sudden urge to go home? My mother (Mom) called a couple of days earlier to let me know that my father had been hospitalized with a collapsed lung. This came as no surprise, because his lungs had collapsed several times in the past and he recovered without complications; but this time there was something unsettling about the tone of Mom's voice. My husband didn't ask any questions. He got up a few hours later and purchased my airline ticket. I packed my bags and, unbeknownst to me, we were off to the airport—the first step of the process for me to close the final chapter of a 30+ year diary.

Almost 10 years earlier, my father had left Mom to return to live with his mother, as he had said for years that he wanted to go back with his parents and run the farm—regardless of Mom's desires. His father had died two or three years before. Shortly after I married, Mom divorced my father.

My father was hospitalized at the Veterans Administration (VA) hospital in a small town near Nashville. It was a beautiful sunny afternoon when I landed at the Nashville airport, which was approximately 15 minutes from the hospital. So I told Mom before I left my home that I would go straight to the hospital when I arrived, and would come to her home after visiting my father. Mom was scheduled to work, so that made sense to me, and she was ok with my plan. As I prepared to leave the rental car garage, I felt an urge to call Mom to make sure she had gone to work. The phone rang a couple times before she answered. I couldn't explain why I felt the urge to call her at home when I knew she should have been at work, and she couldn't explain why she felt the urge to stay home and wait for me. So what did I say?: you want to go to the hospital with me? And, of course, she responded, Yes. It would take over an hour to pick up Mom and return to the hospital, but it was apparent that she wanted to accompany me, so I headed to her home.

Mom mentioned that one of my sisters had also come home to visit him as well, so we agreed to go to the hospital together.

We arrived at the VA Hospital ICU shortly before 3:00 p.m., and as we entered our father's room we saw what appeared to be hundreds of tubes attached to his body that dripped fluids into bags; a breathing apparatus; and, monitors everywhere. My sister and I slowly inched to his bedside so as not to accidently unplug anything, while Mom stood quietly on the opposite side of his bed watching all the monitors (she is a retired licensed practical nurse) as we eased into a small space next to him.

His eyes were closed and I didn't want to startle him, so I softly called out, "Daddy". His eyes started to move around under his eyelids. So again I softly said "Daddy, it's Big Mama" (what he called me). He slowly opened his eyes and turned his head slightly in the direction of my voice. I asked if he could hear me and he nodded his head yes. Then I let him know that Mom and my sister were in the room with me, and he nodded his head to acknowledge that he heard me. I gently touched his arm then softly said, "I Love You." Within a minute or so, tears started to stream from his eyes as he nodded his head multiple times to acknowledge that he heard me. My sister also spoke softly to him, and he nodded his head to acknowledge that he heard her, and shortly thereafter he closed his eyes. We stood quietly staring at him and observed the medical team come into the room, and they asked us to step out for a few minutes. Mom knew what had happened, but she didn't tell us - our father had just passed away.

It was at this moment that I knew why I had to go see him - I had been released. For over 30 years I had been held hostage to the emotional challenges associated with living with an alcoholic parent. The loss of confidence, low self-esteem, fear of failure, helplessness, loneliness, anxiety, and more, were the lingering symptoms of the emotional abuse I endured from having to grow up in a household with an alcoholic parent. The daily arguments, false accusations, profanity, and threats of physical abuse from a parent were very difficult to understand when I didn't know what—if anything I, Mom, or my siblings had done wrong to cause my father to behave in such a hateful manner.

During the time of my presence at his bedside and after the official pronouncement of his death, I realized that I allowed my father to hold me hostage emotionally for all those years. So many children and adults are unaware that they are allowing their past to hold them hostage and, as a result, many become over-, and some under-achievers. It restricts their ability to move forward and use the many God-given gifts and talents for His divine purpose. Take a moment to reflect on a significant emotional event that occurred in your life and try to recall the emotions you felt at that time. Now reflect on a recent experience where something is said or done to you and you respond based on the emotions triggered by the current situation. Did you respond to the current situation or your past experience? You thought you had moved forward, but maybe not.

Some of us become driven because we want to prove to the world that we are better than those around us may think. Some of us are considered under-achievers because we have so many excuses not to use the knowledge and skills with which God has blessed us. Many fear failure and the prospect of negative people saying, "I told you so."

We departed my father's room, and briefly from the hallway, observed the medical team check the tubes and monitors until they pulled the curtains, and we could no longer see him. We then slowly walked to the waiting room while glancing over our shoulders. After 10 to 15 minutes, the medical team came to the waiting area and told us that our father had passed. We all stood silent for a moment then acknowledged the news, which did not come as a surprise. We asked if we could have one final visit with him, which the medical team allowed. As I approached his bedside, I felt a sense of peace and sadness instead of the anger and frustration I had felt towards him for so many years. Had I truly forgiven him?

Unaware of what others in the room were doing at that time, I looked at my father and started to have flashbacks of my experiences with him, but I could recall few memories of a sober father. The same sister who was with me at his bedside was the same sister that was at my side when we were screaming and crying for my Father to get off of Mom after coming home drunk and physically abusing her, even though she was XX months pregnant. That's the earliest and most vivid memory that I have of my father; and it has haunted me for many years. My sister and I were five- and six-years old, respectively when this occurred; and I remember that we cried to the point of exhaustion. We felt so helpless - we couldn't make him stop. To hear Mom's faint voice, the same woman standing at his bedside that day, asking him to please get off of her. It still saddens me to this day. Imagine a child carrying that memory and emotional burden from that day forward? In my mind, I failed to protect my mother. To fail or fear to fail at anything became a trigger for me. Consequently, I was held prisoner for many years until I started to understand more about Mom's faith.

Despite all of the physical and emotional abuse we experienced with my father, Mom, who accepted Christ at a very early age, started to share her faith with us as early as I can remember. She took us to church, and if she couldn't go with us, she made sure we had a way to church until we were old enough to go on our own. Mom not only taught us, but she also modeled the two primary tenants of Christianity, love and forgiveness. I asked, as I'm sure so many others have asked, why would God allow this to happen to us? And how can you love someone that has done so many mean things to you and other family members?

Mom helped me to understand that God requires us to love the sinner but hate the sin. In other words, we were to love our father and others but hate their sinful behavior. I then asked myself how in the world can you separate the two, and the Holy Spirit helped me realize that I can't; only God, through the Holy Spirit, can help me make that separation.

It's not what you say, but what you do. It was my Mom's behavior that caused me to trust her, even when none of this made sense to me. I knew I could not love, forgive, and pray for my father and mean it; so I had to trust that the same God who brought Mom through each encounter with my father would turn the anger and frustration that I felt towards him into love and forgiveness. I had to rely on God to grow me to that point. In time He made it clear to me at my father's bedside that He had replaced all of those negative emotions I felt towards my father with love.

The drive home from the hospital became a time of praise and thankfulness in my heart. God had taken me through a healing process and used prayer and faith to circumcise my heart and remove the negative emotions that had hidden the key to my escape from my past, which were love and forgiveness.

My Mother never taught us against our Father. She encouraged us to love and pray for him because we saw and experienced the destructive effects of what alcohol or any addiction can do to a person; and my father desperately needed help. This is probably one of the main reasons I don't drink today. My father never acknowledged his drinking problem, which is not uncommon for anyone with an addiction. I recall many nights hearing my Mom pray, but I couldn't make out her words through her tears; but she subsequently shared with us when we talked about our past that she prayed ceaselessly for God to protect us from all hurt, harm, and danger; and to allow her to live long enough to see all of her eight children grow up and be able to take care of themselves. She is 91 years old as I write this story; so we remind her that we're not self-sufficient yet, so she'll be around many more years.

My Father, a voracious reader and gifted orator, who also possessed a phenomenal memory. He even professed to have been called to preach. Why did he choose alcohol and deceive himself that worldly pleasures were more important than using his numerous God-given gifts and talents to succeed in life and take care of his family? Was the consumption of alcohol a symptom of other underlying emotional issues that he had not dealt with or was even aware of?

It took years for me to recognize the symptoms of my emotionally abusive childhood. That is why I challenge others today
to assess certain behavior to help them become self-aware that
they may be experiencing symptoms of past experiences that they
have not dealt with, which has been eye-opening for many as it
was for me. Once realized, the main challenge is how to resolve
those issues in your heart so you can move forward with your life.
Each situation is different, and some of us will take longer than
others to turn the doorknob only to realize that the door is not
locked. I contend that the key to moving forward is to honestly
want to let go of your past, which so many people don't really
want to do. Letting go of our past removes the excuses. It wasn't
until I was at that crossroad that I could appreciate the power of,
the need for, and the application of love and forgiveness.

It was a somber morning. We're back to where it all began: the
little country town of Blanche, aka Delrose, Tennessee. We're in
our family church that our paternal grandparents founded, and
where I and most of my siblings accepted Jesus as our Lord and
Savior. I looked at the current pew which replaced the one I sat
on that night during Revival when I joined our family church. At
the end of Revival week, my father assisted the pastor with my
and other new Christians' baptism in a creek called "Kelly's Creek",
which wasn't far from where we lived.

My siblings and I sat quietly during my father's funeral service,
but I didn't sense the urge or emotion to cry as did a couple of my
siblings. Our cousins preached, prayed, and sang, and our godbrother sang and played the piano. I recall our godbrother singing,
"I Don't Feel No Ways Tired" by the Reverend James Cleveland,
which goes like this: "I don't feel no ways tired; come too far from
where I started from; nobody told me, the road would be easy; I
don't believe He brought me this far to leave me", which I believe
was more appropriate for me at that time. I recalled several fu-
nerals in our family church when I was a child. My father helped

with the services to include helping to dig the graves, and now he was the recipient of the same services he provided to others. This is where it started and ended for my father, and where it started for me but also transitioned me to new spiritual heights.

I recall listening to Christian radio en route to work one morning. The Pastor taught about how God created us with a spirit of desire, a desire for Him. Unfortunately many of us misunderstand this scripture and seek to satisfy our desires through earthly pleasures, which are temporary at best. Then the vicious cycle starts again because we are unfulfilled. This can lead to addictive and other destructive behavior and health problems because most people don't understand what's going on. I use my experience and this example to help others become self-aware of what could become self-destructive behavior that can destroy individuals, families, and relationships if they don't address the baggage of the past.

As they lowered my father's casket into the vault, I recalled Mom sharing with me that during her visit with him prior to my arrival in Nashville, he told her that he and God were ok. At one point in my life, I would have responded, oh, really? But I smiled to myself as I watched the funeral attendants adjust the straps to continue to slowly lower his casket into the vault and thought about the prodigal's father who celebrated because his son, who was dead, lived; and was lost, but now was found. (Luke 15:23-24), which tells us that we can repent and return to God through Jesus as our Lord and Savior at any point in our life. I hoped my father was sincere.

About the Author

Ms. Cynthia G. Snyder has served over 36 years in the Federal Government, to include 25 years in the United States Air Force, where she held multiple leadership and command positions prior to her retirement in the grade of Colonel. She earned a Bachelor of Science degree in Civil Engineering from Tennessee State University, Nashville, Tennessee; a Master of Science Degree in Operations Management from the University of Arkansas, Jacksonville, Arkansas campus; and a Master of Science Degree in National Resource Strategy from National Defense University, Fort Lesley McNair, Washington, District of Columbia.

Her portfolio includes vast experience in engineering, facilities management, environmental planning, force protection, emergency management, financial management, transportation planning, logistics management, human capital programs, congressional relations, public affairs, contract management, food service operations, event planning, leader development, and much more, which has garnered her numerous civilian awards and military decorations.

Mrs. Snyder enjoys teaching, reading, writing, cooking, sports, and the Arts. She played a lead role in the recently released independent feature film, Inexplicable Epiphanies, which was written and produced by Mr. Stephen Foreman of Richmond, Virginia. She is in the final stages of producing her first film, which she plans to release in 2017. She plans to continue writing with a focus on how she overcame numerous challenges throughout her personal and professional life, which she hopes will inspire others to never give up.

She is a member of Bethlehem Baptist Church in Alexandria, Virginia, and is an active member of several church ministries to include Church School where she has taught multiple ages and currently teaches elementary age children. She is also a member of the Women's Ministry, and the Worship and Fine Arts Ministry where she is the chorographer for the Women and Children's Dance Ministries.

Ms. Snyder actively supports a number of professional and service organizations and is an active member of the Alpha Kappa Alpha Sorority Inc.

She is married USAF Colonel (retired) Mr. William T. Snyder and they have two daughters, Ara and Charity. She and her family reside in Northern Virginia.

"Your purpose reveals your passion and your passion reveals your heart! Never allow someone [else] to prevent your purpose to blossom into all that it was created to be!

C. Denise

Chapter 9

Created with Purpose...on Purpose
Finding Purpose Through the Pain
Tina Tatum

Have you ever been awake at sunrise? I don't mean those times where you set your alarm and jump up with anticipation to see the sunrise, but rather, a night that finally breaks into day. To see darkness slip away into the aurora of very early morning as the dawn slowly begins to break through to reveal the dew still on the ground, to reveal that you have been blessed with yet another day to live, *another day that you get to choose to live, on purpose.*

I clearly remember that morning. It comes to me in the form a song every now and then that goes something like this, "I can see clearly now the rain is gone...." You know the song. In that moment, however, I did not see things very clearly at all. In fact, instead of seeing the beauty of morning and the dew on the ground, the only sparkle I saw was that of daylight glistening on the lines of cocaine that lay on my living room coffee table. That morning found a young, blonde, 27 year old, married, life of the party, marketing executive that should have been at the prime of her life in pits of sudden destruction. You cannot always judge a book by its cover. I had it all together on the outside, yet on the inside I was dying. I sat there in the stillness of morning staring at those lines when suddenly light broke into my darkness. From somewhere inside I heard these words, "choose life or choose death". I didn't ever feel that I would overdose, rather that this was a crossroads; a doorway if you will. A doorway to either destruction or destiny. *Perhaps a path to find purpose in my pain.*

What I didn't know in the early hours of that morning, that I do know now, is that it would indeed be the first day of the rest of my life, the rising of the sun that day would be the beginning of the end of an eleven-year struggle. That morning everything changed! Understand that *your current situation is not your future destination!*

Go with me for a moment to the genesis of this journey.

I was born into a working middle class family, the youngest of four and the "baby" of the family. My Dad was a hardworking riverboat man and my Mom worked local factory jobs once I started school to help provide for all four us kids to attend private Catholic school from kindergarten through eighth grade. I had a great childhood. I always felt loved, provided for, and safe. As with most teenagers, I began to explore and love my new found freedom in public high school. I had great friends, even one who always told me, "Jesus loves you." However, being the type A personality and leader that I am, I even lead my friends down paths that ended us up in jail in high school, trouble with teachers and parents, and into unhealthy relationships with the opposite sex! Yes, you guessed it, the boyfriend! For brevity of this chapter we will say that always having a need for attention, drinking, and hormones were not a good combination! At the age of 16 I found myself believing that I was in love and pregnant. "Love" had been awakened before its time. My world as I knew it was about to come crumbling down.

In the 80's teen pregnancy and being pregnant outside of marriage was not as prevalent as it is today to say the least. I so feared the rejection of my Dad and family that the only option that I felt I had was abortion. The guy who had told me he loved me only confirmed that his family would feel the same. I remember working for ten weeks to earn enough money for the procedure. Something completely shut down on the inside of me during that time.

I was choosing to kill the very image of God growing on the inside of me. I had never felt more alone. My loneliness had nothing to do with not having people around or even people who loved me. I simply bought into the lie of the enemy, who comes to steal, kill and destroy, that I was a failure and would not be accepted or loved for this mistake; by people or God. I felt my failure was final. I knew abortion was murder, and from my skewed understanding of Catholicism, I believed because I choose death, I was indeed going straight to hell! I made a decision that year, that if I were going to hell anyway, why not just bust the gates wide open?? Of course my relationship with the boyfriend soon died also. Not long after, I found myself going from drink to drink, weed to pills to cocaine, from man to man, from bed to bed until one day I found myself drunk on a beach in Mexico saying "Yes" to a man I would marry only to divorce six years later.

What a waste, Right? This very notion is what lead to an eleven year daily alcohol and drug dependency. I was a functioning addict, still the life of the party, advancing in my career and aging in years. A life spinning out of control, I found myself at "that morning", which I shared at the beginning of this chapter, now facing the reality of an adulterous husband and yet another failure, my marriage. Another disappointment, another rejection. Once again I bought into the lie that I was all alone and that no one would love or accept another piece of damaged goods. **BUT GOD!**

If you find yourself in this same place or in the years of aftermath, do not buy into the lie that I did! I am here to shine the light on the lie that causes isolation and extreme guilt. You are loved and there is forgiveness and healing available to you through Jesus Christ!

Back to the beginning of my story...the sun did rise that morning! And my praying sister was there to lead me to a path of healing and recovery. I took one step out of darkness and one step into the **LIGHT!** I found purpose; not in my life, but in HIS life found in me. You see, *the purpose of your life is greater than your life!* When the center of your life is you, its end is not fulfilling! In the days, months, and years to come I came to know Jesus not only as Savior, but as the healer of the broken hearted, as a friend that sticks closer than a brother, as my deliverer, my peace, my sure foundation, my Lord and the lover of my soul! I also came to know myself as forgiven, accepted in the Beloved, the Apple of His eye, washed in the Blood, saved, set apart, sanctified, justified and far from alone!

Winston Churchhill once said *"Success is not final, failure is not fatal; it is the courage to continue that counts."*

One of my favorite chapters in the Bible is Psalm 139. Check out the reality of what God has to say about you!

O LORD, You have searched me and known me.
2 You know my sitting down and my rising up;
You understand my thought afar off.
3 You comprehend my path and my lying down,

And are acquainted with all my ways.
4 For there is not a word on my tongue,
But behold, O LORD, You know it altogether.
5 You have hedged me behind and before,
And laid Your hand upon me.
6 Such knowledge is too wonderful for me;
It is high, I cannot attain it.
7 Where can I go from Your Spirit?
Or where can I flee from Your presence?
8 If I ascend into heaven, You are there;
If I make my bed in hell, behold, You are there.
9 If I take the wings of the morning,
And dwell in the uttermost parts of the sea,
10 Even there Your hand shall lead me,
And Your right hand shall hold me.
11 If I say, "Surely the darkness shall fall on me,"
Even the night shall be light about me;
12 Indeed, the darkness shall not hide from You,
But the night shines as the day;
The darkness and the light are both alike to You.
13 For You formed my inward parts;
You covered me in my mother's womb.
14 I will praise You, for I am fearfully and wonderfully made;[b]
Marvelous are Your works,
And that my soul knows very well.
15 My frame was not hidden from You,
When I was made in secret,
And skillfully wrought in the lowest parts of the earth.
16 Your eyes saw my substance, being yet unformed.
And in Your book they all were written,
The days fashioned for me,
When as yet there were none of them.
17 How precious also are Your thoughts to me, O God!

How great is the sum of them!

18 If I should count them, they would be more in number than the sand;

When I awake, I am still with You.

Aren't you glad that you were on His mind, long before He was on your mind! You see, God's plans are for your good, even in the midst of poor decisions He will never leave you and He totally understands. He is always there waiting to redirect, waiting to restore! Once you know the truth, it will surely set you free!!! Each one of us is created with purpose and destiny on the inside. Purpose and destiny formed in our DNA long before those strands came together to form our person. Uniquely knit together by our Heavenly Father before the foundations of the earth where even created! Isn't that mind blowing??

You are not an afterthought! You were created with purpose.... And on purpose!

Purposed: to stay in Purpose: Even with all of that truth, all of that assurance through His Word, I am often asked the question; "How do you keep on keeping on?" "How do you do this thing, practically?" To which often answer, "It is a moment, by moment, choice by choice, yes by yes, day by day journey of walking with Jesus!". Often times for the new to come the old must go! Using the analogy of farming, a seed must go into the ground and die before the life grows anew from that seed. At one point in my journey into freedom and purpose I had only two friends, Jesus and my sister, Anita! Some relationships just have to GO! Some will be removed for a season and some will uprooted and removed for a lifetime.

Because our God is also a loving Father He knows what will produce growth in our lives and what will lead to death, so he prunes! The Bible tells us in John 15:1-2 that "I (Jesus) am the true vine, and My Father is the vinedresser. Every branch in Me that does not bear fruit He takes away; and every branch that bears fruit He prunes, that it may bear more fruit" We go through pruning whether we are producing fruit (healthy) or not producing (unhealthy)! Keep in mind that the pruning is always done with the fruit in mind! You will produce when you are in purpose! It brings great joy to the heart of The Father to see you succeed! You may be reading this and have a hard time believing in a good Father who wants all of this for your life. You may not have had a very good example of that in an earthly father. And that's ok, Your Heavenly Father understands times of unbelief, He understands that we are a work in progress. Take one day at a time and choose to trust Him, The One who does not change, The One who will never let you down. I promise your faith will grow and you will grow!

It has been said that "Successful people do daily what unsuccessful people are unwilling to do." I am not real certain where that statement originated from, but I do know from personal experience that it is 100% true! Whether you are a CEO or a stay at home Mom, struggle with body image or drugs and alcohol, whether youre addicted to porn or are addicted to prayer. Small things done daily become habits and habits become a lifestyle that will either lead to freedom or bondage! Life or death! Choose THIS day whom you serve needs to remain on the forefront of our minds as we walk in purpose! Let me share with you a few daily disciplines that have helped me continue to walk in freedom and purpose for the last 18 years.

Finding Jesus! Truly having a personal relationship with my Creator, lover of my soul, healer, friend that sticks closer than a brother and Lord, not a form of religion but a life giving relationship. Spending time in The Word of God and prayer as a matter of priority in my day are a must! And please do not think you are going to read the entire Bible or an entire book every morning! It does not require five hours of prayer to start your day! Or maybe some days it will!! My point is to enjoy sitting down with Jesus in the morning. He is the living Word and as you read the Words of Scripture, and have dialogue (prayer) with Him; What starts out as a discipline will become a delight! My very first Pastor always said, "You will either prepare for your day or you will repair at the end of your day". Words of wisdom to this day!

Relationship with Jesus is paramount and must remain central in our life for all of our life. This vertical relationship will empower us to have healthy horizontal relationships! I often visualize my life in the Cross, literally. For a moment, visualize in your mind's eye, the Cross. The beam that is vertical, ascending up and down represents my relationship with God and the cross beam that runs horizontal represents my earthly relationships; they must all run through the Cross! Make it a point to seek out Godly relationships with those of the same sex as you are walking out your healing and you grow throughout all of life! Spiritual mothers and sisters are vital to our healing and growth. They offer accountability, direction and wisdom for our walk. Because these mentors and leaders in our lives are in a different season they help point out pitfalls and guide us through Biblical and life counsel that is priceless! You must seek these relationships out! Find a prayer group (not a gossip session) Find a Bible Study, a women's group, watch, observe and then seek out these relationship! They will be lifesavers and become treasures in your life for years to come! One more point on relationships. We all have something to give. I have also made it a point, in my life, to not only seek out relationships that deposit life in to me, but to also seek out and be willing to invest in the life of another. There is always someone who is watching you. There is someone that you are ahead of in this journey, maybe only one step, but still you have something of worth to give! In doing so we become what Jesus called "living waters" flowing, receiving and giving of the grace of this life will ensure that our lives do not become stagnant! Our riches truly are in our relationships!

One final area that I would like to address in the process of purpose is that of our mouth! Yes! That thing on the front of your face, that once it releases words, cannot be turned around! There is life and death in the power of the tongue. There are many scriptures that deal with this matter and I recommend that you study them out. Our words frame our world! Be careful how you use them with others and with yourself. It is vital that our words impart life and build up rather than tear down. Many reading this chapter now may have been victims of harsh words growing up, or in a marriage, to this day you can remember the sting of those words. Words fly like arrows and pierce the heart of the intended recipient, for good or for bad. To this day, every morning as I am getting ready for the day, looking in the mirror I speak words to myself! I remind myself of who I am, whose I am and what He has to say about me! Sometimes we just have to say "Self you can't stay here any longer" or "Self you have to move on." Life giving words imparted to you own life, to the life of your husband, children, friends and family can shift the entire climate of your life! You are created with purpose and destiny! You are blessed in the city and blessed in the country, everything you set your hands to is blessed! You are more than a conqueror in Christ Jesus!

Now let me smear a little icing on that cake! He is such a good Father, that after all of the trauma and healing that you read about earlier, God sent me an amazing man, the love of my life, my husband Alan, and blessed us with our daughter Faith and I even get a bonus child in Kyle LaRue! A double portion blessing! Alan and I have shared our own fill of trials and tests in this now seventeen-year journey together. Through it all He has turned our tests into testimonies and our mess in to a ministry to reach out to others!

The purpose that was revealed through all of that pain has come as we pour back into the lives of others. As we lead our family and a generation in knowing who they are in Christ and setting firm foundations that will not be shaken when hard times hit. You see, it's not our job to determine what our purpose is, but rather to discover it through the process of life and in the reflection of His Word! As my very own life was reached, rescued, and redeemed; I find this to be my very same calling to others. Whether it's on the streets to a young girl feeling isolated and with no hope, to the addict believing they will always be so, or from the pulpit to a room full of women needing to be established in their identity. The purpose we have found is the purpose that we are called to shake this world! If we allow it, the very thing that the enemy intends for destruction, God will use for His glory; becoming a stream of life and healing to all those we encounter.

About the Author

Tina Tatum is a lover of Jesus Christ, Wife to Alan, and Mom to Faith and Kyle. By dedicating her life to the calling of family, prayer, preaching, teaching, and advocating for justice, Tina has been promoted to a prominent seat within the local community; while elevated onto global platforms of various movements, ministries, government agencies and corporations.

Tina's ultimate calling is to lay firm foundations for people to follow Jesus Christ with passion, and to arise with courage as an agent of change on the Earth. With a true heart for freeing captives, both physically and spiritually, Tina's purpose always circles back to her primary focus: Sharing Jesus with the world. Tina hosts RefresHER as a faith based series of conferences, conversations and retreat's to minister to and "refresh the lady who refreshes others".

Tina and Alan Co-Founded R3 The Movement, an anti-human trafficking organization that seeks to Reach, Rescue and Redeem those affected by sexual exploitation and slavery. As an overcomer of personal trauma, alcohol and drug addiction herself, she has committed her life to seeing others set free through the power of Jesus!

As Founder of One Voice – Mississippi, a non-denominational, multi- racial, cross-generational admonishment to intercede for the region and nation, Tina provides yet another initiative to compliment and invoke the infrastructure of prayer for the mission of R3 The Movement; one of many collaborative groups, conferences and movements available in Tina's spiritual toolbox for others to utilize freely.

Tina serves as the DeSoto County Chairperson for the National Day of Prayer. She is also recognized as the Apostolic Prayer Leader for the State of Mississippi for US Reformation Prayer Network (USRPN), under the covering of Dr. Cindy Jacobs.

Tina carries a heavy anointing in ministry, and displays integrity in the marketplace. She is recognized by many, exemplified by her life, and amplified by God to fulfill her purpose based on Biblical principles.

www.tinatatum.com
tinamtatum@gmail.com
901-286-1910
Tina Tatum Ministries, R3 The Movement, RefresHER.US
FB_tinatatum: Twitter and Instagram
R3_themovement Twitter

"When purpose awakens, she accomplishes much!"

C. Denise

Chapter 10

Purpose in Connection
Teresa Velardi

Everything? Anything? I can do ALL things? Really? That's what the Word says. I believe that we are each put here on purpose for a purpose by a purposeful God. We were each given gifts and talents to be used like no other person can use them. Those gifts, used with gratitude, are the keys to our lives, abundant lives, while we are here on earth. God watches over us every moment of every day in hopes that we will put him first and know the power and the purpose he has given each of us as we use those gifts in a way that pleases Him.

Each of us has different gifts, so that we can support, complement and help each other. I don't think He meant for any of us to walk this journey alone, or we would be the only person on the planet and we would have **ALL** the gifts ourselves. What good would that do? There would be no one to share them with, or enjoy them with. So we are not alone, ever! Even when there are no people around, God is always with us, encouraging us, if we let him. He brings people into our lives that we can best associate with, collaborate with and together, we can make a difference. That's what connection is about.

There are different kinds of connection. The "word nerd" in me will, of course go to the dictionary for a definition of connection. So, my good friend, with whom I have an ongoing relationship, Webster's dictionary, provides me with this simple definition (please note that I added the word 'people' to this definition):

- something that joins or connects two or more things or people
- the act of connecting two or more things or people, or the state of being connected
- a situation in which two or more things or people have the same cause, origin, goal, etc.

Each of these parts of the definition of connection can be seen in the two major areas of life where we are connected.

Divine Connection

My first connection on a daily basis is with God. It is my spirit (something that joins two or more things) that connects me to Him. In this case, my spirit is joined to the spirit of the creator, God. We are each a part of Him, created in His image, and He desires more than anything else to have a relationship with us. I want a relationship with Him; who gave His only Son, Jesus to die for my sins, who is the way, the truth and the life, therefore I make it my business to make a daily connection with Him. Each morning, I spend time in the word, and in pages written about the word. It's my morning conversation over coffee with God. And it is a conversation. I have heard the whisper of his voice in my heart many times, and have learned, sometimes the hard way, to pay attention and to be obedient to His voice and what He is teaching or how He is directing me. My life is always better when I pay attention to His voice.

Without that morning time, I find that I am scattered, less peaceful, and sometimes without direction. It is the connection to God and with God that inspires me. That time inspires my writing and brings my creative spirit to everything I do. My morning time with Him also inspires and creates space for my connection to other people. By the way, the meaning of the word "inspire" is "In Spirit," so everything I am inspired to do or say, is a blessing from God.

Human Connection

Self Connection

If you're like most people living life at warp speed, I'm sure you are the last person you get in touch with every day. I know this because that's my experience, and most people I talk to, especially women, admit to the same.

The place from which we ideally give to others is from our overflow. Overflow indicates abundance, and God wants us to live life abundantly. When we are not "filling up our cup," there is no overflow. What can you do to connect to yourself? Your body, mind and spirit are connected to each other. Anything we do to increase one, increases all. Need some suggestions?

- Take a walk or go for a run
- Create some powerful I AM statements and practice saying them to yourself in the mirror daily.

- Spend some time journaling paying special attention to gratitude. List at least 3 things or people you are grateful for and experience the feeling of being grateful.
- Color! I find that coloring (I particularly like Mandalas) focuses my mind and opens my vision. Many ideas have flowed to and through me as I watch the colors bring the page to life.
- Treat yourself to a spa day. Whether you go for a massage, a mani-pedi, or sit in the bathtub at home with some candles and your favorite music, this is a great way to relax and connect to you!

Taking time to connect to yourself will "fill your cup" and it will change the way you connect to others.

Connection to Others

One of many gifts that God has given me is the ability to connect with people, heart to heart, soul to soul. For as long as I can remember, I have always been what some refer to as a "people person." I'm the one who knew everyone, the one who could be part of every different group and "fit in." I say this as I reflect back to my high school days. My graduating class was only 103 as the first class graduating from a small town school. We were together, most of us anyway, since early elementary school. We knew each other pretty well, and today, many years later, I still keep in touch with some of those people. We knew the meaning of friendship, and we knew how to collaborate to make things happen (the act of connecting two or things or people, or the state of being connected.) Now that I think about it, this ability for me to connect to people and to connect people to each other has always been part of my life. It's one of those gifts that God gave me.

One to one connection with people requires a few skills to be effective for both parties, whether we are talking about friendship, romantic relationship or business relationships. These skills are important for ALL relationships.

- Be a Good Listener
- Be Authentic
- Don't judge, use good judgment instead
- Say what you mean and mean what you say, but don't say it mean.

Be a Good Listener

In today's worldly super-fast pace of living, we are all moving on to "the next thing" and tend to be three steps ahead of where we actually are. Being a good listener requires us to slow down and more importantly, to be present with whoever it is we are listening to. Let's face it, we ALL want to be heard, but listening and hearing are two different things. We might hear someone say something to us, but didn't connect with the meaning of what was said. The connection comes in the listening. In listening to and for what the person may be feeling, saying with purpose, or needing, we learn how we can be of service to that person. Yes, service. When we are listening, we are doing a service for that person and to God by holding space for them to be heard.

Sometimes in the listening, we will learn something which may be of service to us too. Let's say, as a quick example, you just met someone and they are telling you about their life and their work. As you are listening, they say they have a lawn maintenance business. Just yesterday the person who was maintaining your lawn quit. Now here you are, connecting with someone who could potentially be the one to step into the job. Had you not made that connection, you might never have known. Personally, I think that's a God thing. He fills all our needs. We can indeed do all things through Christ, who not only strengthens us, but blesses us with connections to those who have the ability to do things we don't by using the gifts and talents they are blessed with.

Again, we were never meant to walk this journey alone and although God is always with us, if we were meant to walk alone, He would never have created Eve. (okay, hold up right there ... that's a whole different conversation.) Strong relationships, no matter if they are personal or business, are so important for us to live healthy, happy and joyous lives.

Love is the greatest gift and purpose that each of us has. Jesus said. *"Love one another. As I have loved you, so you must love one another."* **John 13:34**

Be Authentic

How many of us have "put our best face on" for the sake of someone else, or have been in relationship with someone who has done that then as time goes on, we realize the person is completely different than who they were when you met. Or how about when you realize you were hiding behind a mask when you met someone? For whatever reason, at the moment... you wanted the date, or the job, or the friend, or the whatever, and you showed up as the person who you thought would fit the role. Ask me at another time what it means to be living "a scripted life." Authenticity is truth and both are like cream... they always rise to the top! You're only fooling yourself if you are not living authentically.

There are many scriptures that tell us not to compare ourselves to others and that we are fearfully and wonderfully made in the image of God. Why do we always look to change who we have been created to be by the Creator of all things? Social pressure? Worldly living? I think God wants us to be the best version of who He created us to be all around, at all times. It is from that place, that he gives us the opportunity to connect with others who will walk with us on our journey through life, and it's so much easier that trying to figure things out from a different perspective. Just **BE YOU** authentically.

Don't Judge, Use Good Judgment Instead

Sometimes we pay too much attention to what others are doing and tend to be judgmental when it is "not the right thing" or they are "not doing things the way they should be done." Does this sound familiar? Judgment of others does not build connection, it destroys it. In a recent sermon at my church, the pastor explained Matthew 7:1-6 really well. He said, "use good judgment, but don't be judgmental." The scripture says: If we judge others, we will be judged in the same way. That statement alone has me putting the brakes on. There's a huge difference between being judgmental and using good judgment. When we can discern the difference, we will have closer relationships with people. Our connections to each other will be stronger. Even when we feel the need to discuss a sensitive issue with someone close to us, the way we handle it can make or break the relationship connection. That leads me to the next point in building and maintaining connections with people...

Say What You Mean and Mean What You Say, But Don't Say it Mean

Someone once told me I could get away with saying almost anything as long as I said it with a smile on my face and love in my heart. Remember, we are here to love one another. I do my best to live by what I have written here, and in doing so, have built wonderful, long term relationships. I have had to walk away from some as well, having made a good judgment call for myself. One of those was to divorce my husband. I had made a poor decision, one that I had heard God tell me not to make, but I didn't know it was God's voice at the time. So when I realized what I had truly gotten myself into, having had blinders on at the altar, I had to make a better choice in the end to leave with my son. It was best for all of us.

That's just one example of using my connection to God to make a better choice for myself. In doing so, God has connected me to people who have changed my life in so many wonderful ways. I've paid attention, without questioning, to the whisper of His voice when I hear it.

One of the most recent whispers has to do with this book. I called Dr. C Denise Richardson because God had put it on my heart to share a few things that could be good for each of us to be a part of. In doing so, we decided to share in each other's book projects. I'm so excited to be able to write for this book and she will be a part of my "A Daily Gift of Gratitude" book. Dr. C. recognizes my ability to make connections with people, to create collaboration and to join hearts and forces with other people, mostly women. We girls have to stick together, especially in certain areas of living life, like holding space for nurturing and healing in our bodies, minds, families, friends and communities. We need to connect each other to people who can help us expand our businesses or get our message out to the world in a bigger way.

Today, the most valuable assets we have in our lives, both personal and business, are the relationships we build. Christ has strengthened me in being able to build great connections and relationships. He has also given me courage to step out of the box to see where those connections would be a great fit for others. (a situation in which two or more things or people have the same cause, origin, goal, etc).

God has given us a spirit of courage, just like Joshua! It is through that courage, and being able to connect heart to heart without hesitation to others, that we are able to grow in love for one another. How wonderful would the world be if we all didn't see the color of skin, the shape of eyes, the garments people wear, the money they have in the bank, the religion they practice or the country they live in as a wall or a stop sign to a connection with that person. God created us ALL in His image, and together, we look like a box of crayons.

As I write this, I'm hearing a song in my heart. It's the old Beetles Song, "All You Need is Love." That song was written for a world tour that's purpose was strictly to spread a message of love to the world. People came together to connect with that message as the Beetles toured the world. The message of Jesus, "Love one another" was alive and well and being played on stage by the Beetles, bringing people of the world together.... connecting to the message of love. It may not have been delivered exactly the same, but there was no hate, no violence happening as they shared their message. Love is universal. God is Love... and although there have been many things that are not the perfect picture of love in this world, stay focused on those that are. What you think about becomes your reality. It's biblical...

Romans 12:2 Do not conform to the pattern of this world, but be transformed by the renewing of your mind. Then you will be able to test and approve what God's will is— his good, pleasing and perfect will.

Let the message of love be that which connects you to all the people you want to be part of your message. And if you need a little help, let me know, I'll see if I can connect you with some of the people God has put in my world and will be grateful for the opportunity to do so.

Yes, I can do all things through Christ who strengthens me... and to borrow a line from the Beetles, I get by with a little help from my friends!

About the Author

Teresa Velardi is a leader, author, speaker, publisher and host of Transformational Tuesdays. Living her life in authenticity and gratitude, while making a difference in the lives of others are Teresa's passion and purpose. Knowing that everyone has a story to tell, she is also committed to helping people to share their stories with the world.

As the host of Transformational Tuesdays, Teresa often says that the one thing in life that is constant is change. We are forever changing and growing into the awesome people we were created to be. Also a skilled potter, Teresa often uses the art of making pottery as an illustration for transformation.

To learn more or connect with Teresa go to www.teresavelardi.com.

To register for Transformational Tuesdays and receive a free gift go to www.transformationaltuesdays.com.

For more on sharing your story in an upcoming book, go to www.yourstorymattersnow.com.

Chapter 11

Thirty Days to Purpose: A Purpose Activation Guide

This guide demonstrates faith in action through the Word of God. The central objective of this guide is to provoke both critical thought and intentional action in the area of purpose! During the next thirty days, you will be challenged to act on what you speak and believe concerning your [own] purpose!

Day One

"He has saved us and called us to a holy life—not because of anything we have done but because of his own purpose and grace." (2 Timothy 1:9)

Challenge: Create a list of things you are passionate about and integrate them into your life over the next twelve (12) months. Create a (POA) Plan of Action.

_____
_____
_____
_____
_____
_____
_____
_____
_____
_____
_____
_____
_____
_____
_____
_____
_____
_____
_____
_____
_____
_____
_____

Day Two

"But I have raised you up for this very purpose, that I might show you my power and that my name might be proclaimed in all the earth." (Exodus 9:16)

Challenge: List three things that you "believe" God has called you to do but, they seem too great to achieve and are quite over-whelming. You may not have the resources, assistance, or visibility right now.

_____

_____

_____

_____

_____

_____

_____

_____

_____

_____

_____

_____

_____

_____

_____

_____

_____

_____

_____

_____

_____

Day Three

"The purposes of a person's heart are deep waters, but one who has insight draws them out." (Proverbs 20:5)

Challenge: Create a vision statement that outlines your comprehensive objective. Make it relative to your (POA) Plan of Action.

_____

_____

_____

_____

_____

_____

_____

_____

_____

_____

_____

_____

_____

_____

_____

_____

_____

_____

_____

_____

_____

_____

_____

_____

Day Four

"Therefore, my dear friends, as you have always obeyed—not only in my presence, but now much more in my absence—continue to work out your salvation with fear and trembling, for it is God who works in you to will and to act in order to fulfill his good purpose." (Philippians 2:12-13)

Challenge: Comprise a list of five to seven individuals who have similar interests as you do. Then, select 2-3 to begin collaborating and networking with.

_____
_____
_____
_____
_____
_____
_____
_____
_____
_____
_____
_____
_____
_____
_____
_____
_____
_____
_____
_____
_____
_____
_____

Day Five

"And we know that in all things God works for the good of those who love him, who have been called according to his purpose" (Romans 8:28).

Challenge: List five presumably negative encounters that were **NOT** negative at all! Next, tell how they really helped you in the area of purpose according to Romans 8:28.

_____

_____

_____

_____

_____

_____

_____

_____

_____

_____

_____

_____

_____

_____

_____

_____

_____

_____

_____

_____

_____

_____

_____

_____

Day Six

"Without counsel purposes are disappointed: but in the multitude of counsellors they are established." (Proverbs 15:22)

Challenge: Comprise a list of seven women you respect and with whom you would readily seek counsel. Now, commit to contacting one of them each day for the next seven days.

_____

_____

_____

_____

_____

_____

_____

_____

_____

_____

_____

_____

_____

_____

_____

_____

_____

_____

_____

_____

_____

_____

_____

Day Seven

"Now unto him that is able to do exceeding abundantly above all that we ask or think, according to the power that worketh in us...". (Ephesians 3:20).

Challenge: Jot down a major goal that blesses others and is truly inconceivable **EXCEPT** that God does it through you!

_____

_____

_____

_____

_____

_____

_____

_____

_____

_____

_____

_____

_____

_____

_____

_____

_____

_____

_____

_____

_____

_____

Day Eight

"The LOrd will perfect that which concerneth me: thy mercy, O Lord, endureth for ever: forsake not the works of thine own hands." (Psalm 138:8)

Challenge: Complete a task today that you have previously neglected. C'mon, Just Do It! **#NOW** Hold yourself accountable to act TODAY.

_____
_____
_____
_____
_____
_____
_____
_____
_____
_____
_____
_____
_____
_____
_____
_____
_____
_____
_____
_____
_____

Day Nine

"And be not conformed to this world: but be ye transformed by the renewing of your mind, that ye may prove what is that good, and acceptable, and perfect, will of God." (Romans 12:2)

Challenge: Think of one area in your life that requires change. Now, select the one thing you can change about that situation (maybe your: attitude, perspective, action, fear), and change it. Do it **#NOW**

_____

_____

_____

_____

_____

_____

_____

_____

_____

_____

_____

_____

_____

_____

_____

_____

_____

_____

_____

_____

_____

Day Ten

"The Lord of hosts hath sworn, saying, Surely as I have thought, so shall it come to pass; and as I have purposed, so shall it stand..." (Isaiah 14:24)

Challenge: Develop a brief statement of "purpose" as it relates to your knowledge of this scripture and speaking "life" into oneself. (similar to a mission or vision statement but pertaining more to "purpose").

_____

_____

_____

_____

_____

_____

_____

_____

_____

_____

_____

_____

_____

_____

_____

_____

_____

_____

Day Eleven

"For I know the thoughts that I think toward you, saith the Lord, thoughts of peace, and not of evil, to give you an expected end." (Jeremiah 29:11)

Challenge: Write out seven attributes you think and believe about yourself, (as a covenant agreement to agree with God's word about you).

_____

_____

_____

_____

_____

_____

_____

_____

_____

_____

_____

_____

_____

_____

_____

_____

_____

_____

_____

_____

_____

_____

_____

Day Twelve

"But God hath chosen the foolish things of the world to confound the wise; and God hath chosen the weak things of the world to confound the things which are mighty..." (J Corinthians 1:27)

Challenge: Create a list of five seemingly foolish things that actually proved beneficial to God's purpose for your life (i.e. writing a book, hosting a support group for women, sponsoring a youth empowerment brunch, etc.).

_____

_____

_____

_____

_____

_____

_____

_____

_____

_____

_____

_____

_____

_____

_____

_____

_____

_____

_____

_____

_____

_____

Day Thirteen

"Declaring the end from the beginning, and from ancient times the things that are not yet done, saying, My counsel shall stand, and I will do all my pleasure..." (Isaiah 46:10)

Challenge: Commit to reading one chapter of the Bible per day for twenty-one days. (Stick with the same book for twenty-one days for optimal results. I suggest Psalm, Proverbs or Ephesians).

_____
_____
_____
_____
_____
_____
_____
_____
_____
_____
_____
_____
_____
_____
_____
_____
_____
_____
_____
_____
_____
_____

Day Fourteen

"Wherefore be ye not unwise, but understanding what the will of the Lord is." (Ephesians 5:17)

Challenge: Journal today for fifteen (15) minutes about your feelings **TODAY**.

_____

_____

_____

_____

_____

_____

_____

_____

_____

_____

_____

_____

_____

_____

_____

_____

_____

_____

_____

_____

_____

_____

_____

_____

Day Fifteen

"I said in mine heart, God shall judge the righteous and the wicked: for there is a time there for every purpose and for every work." (Ecclesiastes 3:17)

Challenge: Create a "T-Chart" and list your completed and incomplete goals and objectives from the past five (5) years. **#JudgeYourCommitmentToPurpose** (critic your own level of commitment)

_____

_____

_____

_____

_____

_____

_____

_____

_____

_____

_____

_____

_____

_____

_____

_____

_____

_____

_____

Day Sixteen

"To every thing there is a season, and a time to every purpose under the heaven..." (Ecclesiastes 3:1)

Challenge: Meditate on something fun you'd previously contemplated on experiencing (jet skiing, blogging, speaking on a FB Live, Periscope, or skydiving) and set a timeframe of seven days to sign up or complete the task.

_____

_____

_____

_____

_____

_____

_____

_____

_____

_____

_____

_____

_____

_____

_____

_____

_____

_____

_____

_____

_____

Day Seventeen

"But rise, and stand upon thy feet: for J have appeared unto thee for this purpose, to make thee a minister and a witness both of these things which thou hast seen, and of those things in the which J will appear unto thee..." (Acts 26:16)

CHALLENGE: See what you speak! Speak what you believe! Remember, it's the words we believe that ultimately manifests in our lives. Now, speak life today! Rise and minister (speak the words of God) to yourself! This is a proven benefit termed "affirmations". List 7 beliefs that are your "core".

_____

_____

_____

_____

_____

_____

_____

_____

_____

_____

_____

_____

_____

_____

_____

_____

_____

_____

_____

_____

Day Eighteen

"And the Lord answered me, and said, Write the vision, and make it plain upon tables, that he may run that readeth it." (Habakkuk 2:2)

Challenge: Rewrite (on a vision board) your comprehensive "vision" statement with the use of both words and pictures.

_____

_____

_____

_____

_____

_____

_____

_____

_____

_____

_____

_____

_____

_____

_____

_____

_____

_____

_____

_____

_____

_____

_____

_____

Day Nineteen

"For the vision is yet for an appointed time, but at the end it shall speak, and not lie: though it tarry, wait for it; because it will surely come, it will not tarry." (Habakkuk 2:3)

Challenge: Begin today checking the "benchmarks" of both your attempted and completed goals. *Sit down and create a spreadsheet to complete this task* This requires commitment.

_____
_____
_____
_____
_____
_____
_____
_____
_____
_____
_____
_____
_____
_____
_____
_____
_____
_____
_____
_____
_____

Day Twenty

"So shall my word be that goeth forth out of my mouth: it shall not return unto me void, but it shall accomplish that which I please, and it shall prosper in the thing whereto I sent it." (Isaiah 55:11)

Challenge: Comprise a list of significant accomplishments you are able to celebrate today! Do not include parenting!

_____

_____

_____

_____

_____

_____

_____

_____

_____

_____

_____

_____

_____

_____

_____

_____

_____

_____

_____

_____

_____

_____

Day Twenty-One

"The counsel of the Lord standeth forever, the thoughts of his heart to all generations."
(Psalm 33:11)

Challenge: List three individuals from whom you currently seek counsel. Now, from that same list; eliminate two that should be removed and replaced by two.

_____

_____

_____

_____

_____

_____

_____

_____

_____

_____

_____

_____

_____

_____

_____

_____

_____

_____

_____

_____

_____

_____

_____

_____

Day Twenty-Two

"Even so then at this present time also there is a remnant according to the election of grace. (Romans 11:5)

Challenge: Document in your journal an experience in previous times that you would consider yourself to have been a "remnant". List the individual(s) who assisted you during this time. Define remnant in your journaling.

_____

_____

_____

_____

_____

_____

_____

_____

_____

_____

_____

_____

_____

_____

_____

_____

_____

_____

_____

_____

Day Twenty-Three

"According as he hath chosen us in him before the foundation of the world, that we should be holy and without blame before him in love...". (Ephesians 1:4)

Challenge: Today, before the day ends; demonstrate an intentional act of "Love" by doing something kind for someone you don't know. (i.e., purchase lunch, dinner, fuel, grocery item, etc.) Next, write/journal about it.

_____

_____

_____

_____

_____

_____

_____

_____

_____

_____

_____

_____

_____

_____

_____

_____

_____

_____

_____

_____

_____

Day Twenty-Four

"Having predestinated us unto the adoption of children by Jesus Christ to himself, according to the good pleasure of his will...". (Ephesians 1:5)

Challenge: Answer this question and ask yourself if you are, in fact, living up to both [your] purpose and potential. Well, are you? How does it feel?

_____

_____

_____

_____

_____

_____

_____

_____

_____

_____

_____

_____

_____

_____

_____

_____

_____

_____

_____

_____

_____

_____

Day Twenty-Five

"But as for you, ye thought evil against me; but God meant it unto good, to bring to pass, as it is this day, to save much people alive." (Genesis 50:20)

Challenge: Write an "apology" letter to someone you've thought evil against. This is quite challenging since we often see ourselves as the "victim". This is just for your journal unless you feel compelled to do otherwise.

_____

_____

_____

_____

_____

_____

_____

_____

_____

_____

_____

_____

_____

_____

_____

_____

_____

_____

_____

_____

Day Twenty-Six

"Train up a child in the way he should go: and when he is old, he will not depart from it." (Proverbs 22:6)

Challenge: List an important "purpose" component that you attribute to your teachings as a child.

_____

_____

_____

_____

_____

_____

_____

_____

_____

_____

_____

_____

_____

_____

_____

_____

_____

_____

_____

_____

_____

_____

_____

_____

_____

Day Twenty-Seven

"Now My soul has become troubled; and what shall I say, 'Father, save Me from this hour'? But for this purpose I came to this hour." (John 12:27)

Challenge: Today, focus on something that you were passionate about but did not complete and forgive yourself. Journal about it! How do you feel? Why?

_____

_____

_____

_____

_____

_____

_____

_____

_____

_____

_____

_____

_____

_____

_____

_____

_____

_____

_____

_____

_____

_____

_____

Day Twenty-Eight

"For I have come down from heaven, not to do My own will, but the will of Him who sent Me." (John 6:38)

Challenge: Recount a time that you regret doing your [own] will instead of God's when you knew it would prove detrimental to your life of purpose. Write down your thoughts now looking retrospectively?

_____

_____

_____

_____

_____

_____

_____

_____

_____

_____

_____

_____

_____

_____

_____

_____

_____

_____

_____

_____

_____

Day Twenty-Nine

"And I came this day unto the well, and said, O Lord God of my master Abraham, if now thou do prosper my way which I go..." (Genesis 24:42)

Challenge: List one thing God "prospered" you to do that you have consistently worked on? List one thing has God "prospered" you to do that you have not committed to but desire to? Begin today working toward that objective.?

_____

_____

_____

_____

_____

_____

_____

_____

_____

_____

_____

_____

_____

_____

_____

_____

_____

_____

_____

_____

_____

_____

Day Thirty

"God is not a man, that he should lie; neither the son of man, that he should repent: hath he said, and shall he not do it? or hath he spoken, and shall he not make it good?" (Numbers 23:19)

Challenge: List three promises you've commuted to this year that you have yet to complete. Now, list them in order of priority and complete the first priority within thirty (30) to ninety (90) days.

_____

_____

_____

_____

_____

_____

_____

_____

_____

_____

_____

_____

_____

_____

_____

_____

_____

_____

_____

_____

_____

_____

_____

_____

_____

Chapter 12

Twenty-One Journal Activities to Ignite Purpose

DAYS 1-7: R(EINSTATE) YOUR PURPOSE

Day 1: God began a good work in you. Now, it's dormant, stagnate, impeded. Begin TODAY by gradually reentering that arena that once brought joy and happiness to others as well as to you! List one action you will take toward reinstating your purpose.

Day 2: God's primary purpose for all of His creations is to glorify Himself. List one action you will take today that will reveal God's glory through your purpose initiatives.

Day 3: Purpose is a life long commitment. In order to reinstate your purpose, commitment must be a priority. List seven areas you have lacked commitment with one being in the area of purpose.

Day 4: Purpose requires a plan. What is your plan of action concerning your purpose journey? Remember, Habakkuk 2:2. Now, if you're truly serious about reinstating your purpose; write out your vision. This should excite you and cause your soul to rejoice.

Day 5: Now that you've written the "vision" (Purpose statement), it's time to activate it. Activation requires faith and assistance. List seven individuals you will contact within seven days to assist you with what God has purposed you to do. Remember to pray prior to requesting assistance. God's thoughts differs from ours.

Day 6: Next, set a tentative date that you would like to accomplish each milestone as you continue to rebuild purpose. Time is of the essence! Do not delay or procrastinate in completing this task.

Day 7: Finally, "purpose" is NOT solely for ourselves but rather, for others who will benefit from the gift of God within us. So, who will be blessed by your life of purpose?

DAYS 8-11: (I)NSPIRE YOUR PASSION

Day 8: Passion is said to be the catalyst for purpose! What are you intensely passionate about that inspires you and others? This is like your passion on steroids.

Day 9: What measurable steps do you have set in place to ensure that your purpose continues no matter how you "feel"?

Day 10: Becoming inspired is one thing. Remaining inspired is quite another. The Bible informs us that the race (or predestined outcome) is given to those who persist. Share three inspirational quotes that consistently motivate you.

DAYS 12-17: (C)HANGE YOUR CIRCLES

Day 12: Those whom we keep close company with have the greatest influence and impact in our lives. List the top three influential individuals in your circle today.

Day 13: Create a "RICH" circle list compromised of seven women you'd like to connect with for the following areas of your life: personal, professional, and spiritual.

Day 14: Ask yourself if your circles are "diversity RICH"; not solely in color but professionally as well. If not, create a list of 3 individuals you'd like to include in your circles.

Day 15: List three ways your circle has changed since you have defined "purpose".

Day 16: List three qualities you bring/introduce to your circles.

Day 17: Change requires a mindset shift. Are your prepared to do so today? Now? List one "action" step you're prepared to initiate NOW to demonstrate your commitment.

DAYS 18-21 (H)AVE FAITH IN YOUR GOD

Day 18: Now faith is... How has faith guided your actions regarding "purpose"? In faith, take an "action" step that frightens you (i.e. contact someone you admire who may be able to assist you in launching your idea).

Day 19: Activate faith today by investing in a life, confidence, or relationship coach. Do this today! Go on, have faith in your God!

Day 20: What are your greatest fears concerning "purpose"? Now, begin to truly envision yourself overcoming those fears by engaging in some sort of volunteer participation with a nonprofit. Commit for a minimum of six months

Day 21: Faith is often demonstrated through our actions. Contact a non-profit organization today to invest a nominal monthly seed for six months. Commit to sacrifice a pleasure or vice for six months as a step of faith). **#ActionIsFaith #FaithIsAction**

RICH

Reinstate Your Purpose
Inspire Your Passion
Change Your Circles
Have Faith in Your God

"On Any Given Day...Like the Sun, We Rise to the Call of Purpose." – C. Denise